KU-315-749

REINVENTING
LETTERING

REINVENTING LETTERING

Inspirational pieces by contemporary practitioners

EMILY GREGORY

BLOOMSBURY

LONDON · NEW DELHI · NEW YORK · SYDNEY

First published in Great Britain in 2012

Bloomsbury Publishing Plc.
50 Bedford Square
London
WC1B 3DP
UK

ISBN 978-1-4081-7384-8

Copyright © RotoVision 2012
Text copyright © Emily Gregory 2012

CIP Catalogue records for this book are available from
the British Library and the US Library of Congress.

All rights reserved. No part of this publication may be
reproduced in any form or by any means – graphic,
electronic or mechanical, including photocopying,
recording, taping or information storage and retrieval
systems – without the prior permission in writing of
the publishers.

Emily Gregory has asserted her right under the
Copyright, Design and Patents Act 1988 to be
identified as the author of this work.

Typeset in 7 on 11.6pt Museo Slab

Book design by Emily Portnoi
Layout: Rebecca Stephenson
Cover artwork by Jason Wong
Commissioning Editor: Isheeta Mustafi
Copyeditor: Salima Hirani

Printed in China by 1010 Printing International Ltd.

20/8/14

Leeds College of Art
Library
655
2

R83566F

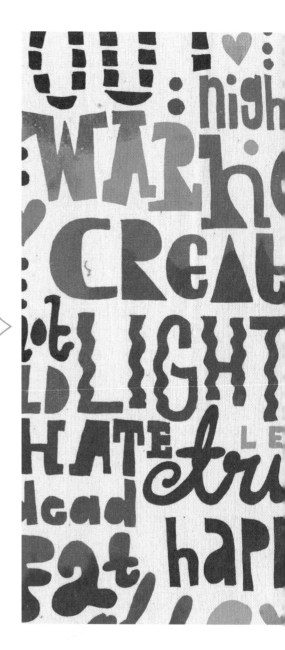

False EVIL ꞮꞮꞮꞮ ꞮꞮꞮꞮ aliv

aven BEGIN enter

LOVE

END MORE WHITE DARK

WHITE i

GOOD Sad

Day DESTRO

CRY HELL young

LAU·

y PEACE ·GH NE

BLACK

CONTENTS

T / t
Tiger Shark

U / u
Unau

P / p
Pinemarten

Z / z
Zeren

INTRODUCTION

Flicking through the pages that follow, it is clear that a global resurgence of lettering is in full swing. Artists and designers, each with their own unique vision and techniques, are working with intent to bring character and new depth to typography. In many examples, the letters do not act merely as captions or supporting visuals, but as images in their own right, enhancing communication and impact. The lettering gives the words a stronger voice and an enhanced visual presence.

In some cases, this renewed love affair with letters represents a movement away from the computer to a more tactile and personal aesthetic; from the perfect and replicable nature of typefaces to what some describe as the 'consistent imperfection' of the human hand. Through crafting individual letters, whether digitally, by hand or three-dimensionally, a new value is added, and the stamp of the artist is made upon the work.

Many of the practitioners featured in this book work with lettering because it allows them to push the boundaries of form. Maintaining legibility, while at the same time creating something new and exciting, is seen both as a challenge and a constraint. Nina Gregier explains, 'You can give letters any shape, but you have to remember about the features of letters, about readability and the principles of building the shape of letters. No matter how funny or strange a letter would have been, you always have to follow these rules.'

Expression, too, is at the crux of much of the work. The visualisation of a word or phrase to add meaning (rather than just to look attractive) becomes all the more valuable as a tool of communication. Dan Cassaro is one practitioner who revels in this task, explaining 'Letters sit squarely between information and meaning so what we choose to do with them is very important and exciting.'

This book showcases the work of some of today's leading practitioners of lettering. As the distinction between image and text continues to blur, there is no denying the value that lettering holds and the endless possibilities for new and exciting things to come in the future.

1 The tools and work space of
Chris Ballasiotes (pages 130–132)
2 A work in progress at the studio
of sign-writing artist Jeff Canham
(pages 110–112)
3 / 4 Josh Luke of Best Dressed
Signs paints in layers on glass
for his vintage-inspired lettering
(see pages 144–147)

Chapter 1:
Digitally Drawn Lettering

Digital lettering allows artists and designers to go beyond the conventions of using fonts to create something exciting and original while still maintaining a professional and clean finish that can sit easily alongside any other type.

Artists and designers practising with digital methods approach their work in a variety of ways. Many begin with sketches in the planning stages – either loose or almost completely resolved – and then scan them in. Retracing these sketches in Adobe Illustrator, they create vector curves that can be easily resized or work over them in Adobe Photoshop to add colour or texture or to composite various elements together.

On the other side of the spectrum are those who complete the entire process on the computer, such as Jessica Hische (see pages 16–19) and Dado Queiroz (see pages 34–35). Some prefer this method as it allows the qualities of the computer program to shape the outcome, or they simply feel it to be a more organic means of production. The use of a graphics tablet is often helpful to mimic the flowing lines of a pen in these cases, although it is not essential.

1

The advantages of digital lettering are many, especially for working on client projects. Hand-lettering practitioners will often complain of the hours taken in revising a piece of work and, although it is not necessarily always simple to amend digitally, it is sometimes not necessary to begin again, as you may have to do if the work was done by hand. This makes working in digital form a popular choice for many; colours can be changed many times, letters can be resized with no loss of quality and, in addition, existing fonts can be easily used as a base if so desired.

Although it may seem that, by using the same programs, digital practitioners may have similar outcomes, this is not true. A computer-illustrated letterform can vary hugely – every bit as much as a pencil drawing. This chapter showcases a broad range of digital artists working with different techniques and producing very individual works.

1 Drawing straight onto the computer with the aid of his graphics tablet, Dado Queiroz (see pages 34 – 35) does not feel the need to make prior sketches
2 The bright studio of Keetra Dean Dixon (see page 23)
3 Jon Contino's well set up studio (see pages 54 – 55)
4 The precise sketches of Alonzo Felix (see page 61) are scanned in and traced in Illustrator to create vector illustrations

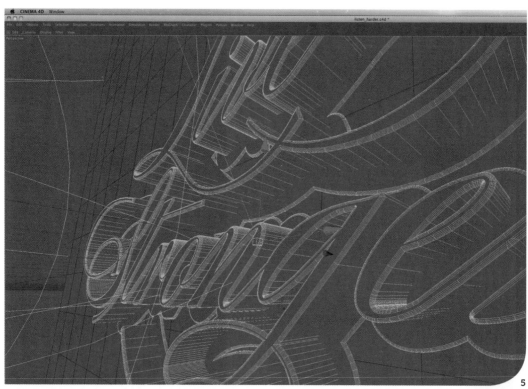

5

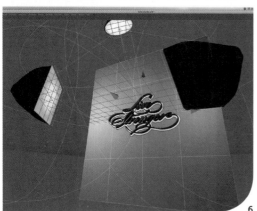

6

7

TOOLS

There are a number of tools, in addition to a computer, that are necessary (or helpful) for digital works.

Scanner

Many practitioners scan their sketches to work over once on the computer. In addition, textures and other elements can be scanned to give work a warmer feel.

Graphics tablet

Using a pen rather than a mouse is, for many, a more free-flowing and natural way of working. Flowing curves and organic line work can be more easily acheived in this way.

Adobe Illustrator (or equivalent)

A vector-based program allows practitioners to work with curves that can be resized without loss of quality.

Adobe Photoshop (or equivalent)

This program allows the addition of colour and texture and can also be used to draw digitally.

FontLab (or equivalent)

For those who wish to create letters to type with, such programs are hugely helpful. To create a fully functioning font, however, you must also design elements such as ligatures and glyphs, for example.

8

9

5 / 6 / 7 / 8 / 9 The use of three-dimensional software, as shown here by Joey Camacho (see page 38), allows even more diversity to be explored within digital lettering

DENNIS PAYONGAYONG

Brooklyn, New York, USA

The Friends of Type (see also pages 15, 70 and 85) is an essential resource for all lettering junkies, and member Dennis Payongayong created these two compositions for the website of this organisation.

He generally scans his rough sketches, drawn on paper with ballpoint pens, cheap mechanical pencils, Pilot Fineliners, brush pens and old Sharpies, and cleans things up in Photoshop or Illustrator.

For Payongayong, the inspiration of the message – a sentence, phrase or word – must be maintained. If he feels the aesthetics are interfering with the message, he will start again. He says, 'It's really tough because, as a designer, I'm drawn to style, but sometimes style is overwhelming.'

1 *You had me at hello*
2 *Change*

14 |

JASON WONG
Brooklyn, New York, USA

Jason Wong is also a member of collective Friends of Type and founder of the well-known stationery and printing company Enormous Champion. He says of the visual stimulation of lettering, 'I love the fact that random shapes and lines can come together to conjure emotions and feelings before the word is communicated.'

The two designs shown here were created for Friends of Type as an escape from client work. They began as sketches and were then developed on the computer using Illustrator and Photoshop. Keep It Tight comes from Wong's fascination with tying knots, while Yesterday's History, Tomorrow's A Mystery (the piece is titled Today's Gift) was created in eager anticipation of becoming a parent.

1

2

3

1 *Keep it tight*
2 *Yesterday's history tomorrow's a mystery*
3 Detail

JESSICA HISCHE

San Francisco,
California, USA

Due to a lack of funds to buy fonts while at college, Jessica Hische soon realised that her hand-drawn type was more effective than any font she could find. She now creates custom lettering for almost every project she works on. Shown here is a range of her work for various clients, as well as her self-initiated Daily Drop Cap alphabets, for which she is so well known.

Hische's initial pencil sketches are completed primarily for the client and, upon digitising them, she will draw again completely fresh. She explains, 'I believe that the translation from sketch to final without tracing helps me correct my mistakes as I go. I idealise, like how you would if you were drawing a person from memory versus from real life.'

When composing a lettering piece, she will first complete the 'skeleton' of the forms before adding any ornaments or decoration (such as the thicks and thins).

1

2

3

1 *Congratulations*

2 *Gift*

3 Alphabet

SUMMER BOOK PREVIEW

4

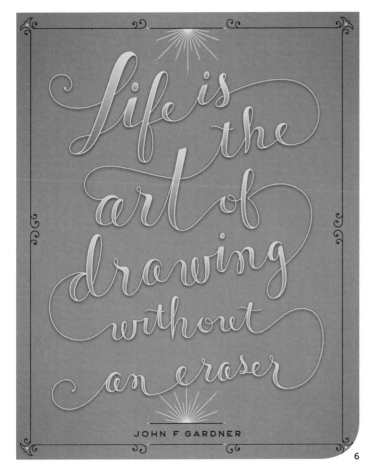

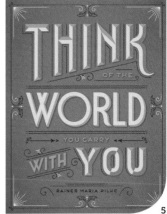

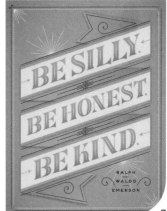

4 *Summer book preview*

5 *Life is the art of drawing without an eraser. John F Gardner*

6 *Think of the world you carry with you. Rainer Maria Rilke*

7 *Be silly. Be honest. Be kind. Ralph Waldo Emerson*

ADAM HILL
Cape Town, South Africa

Although he uses digital techniques to create his lettering works, Adam Hill always begins with sketches of his ideas on paper. He says, 'I believe strongly in thinking with pencil and paper before going on to computer. Even if it means just a few clumsy scribbles, it helps to oil the machine.'

After using a font to help with proportions, he then rebuilds the type in Photoshop using layers, so that each element can be edited in isolation. Hill often adds subtle shadows or noise to enhance the final look.

The piece below was designed to be a repeat-pattern mural for a large financial institution in South Africa. It was inspired by the strong geometric shapes of the Avant Garde and the Mexico 1968 Olympics identity.

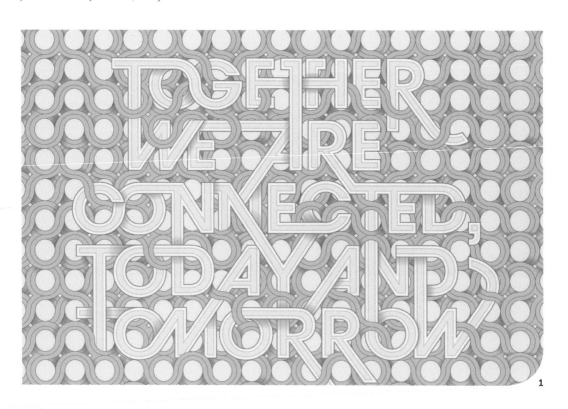

1

2

1 *Together we are connected, today and tomorrow*

2 *Youth is wasted on the young*

DANIELLE DAVIS

Lawton,
Oklahoma, USA

Designer and illustrator Danielle Davis takes great joy from manipulating letterforms to create her pieces. On the subject of what inspires her she says, 'I love words, and I love language. Creating new letterforms is a perfect outlet for me to share that.' This project was a self-promotional piece to send out to clients and friends.

Davis works from start to finish on the computer, using only a mouse to control the pen tool in Illustrator. Restricting herself to just one fine line, she begins with her favourite vowels, then works through the letters, leaving those she finds trickiest (*t* and *s*) until last. Her sweeping curves are refined solely by adjusting Bézier curves, without any help from mathematics.

1

1 *Whoops a daisy*

2 *Bon voyage*

2

KEETRA DEAN DIXON
Baltimore,
Maryland, USA

The work of Keetra Dean Dixon is, at times, abstract and spans many forms of art and design beyond lettering. Experimentation is key and, as such, her process and use of materials change with almost every project. She says, 'A favourite method is one I call digital tool breaking: using familiar tools in unfamiliar ways or ways in which they weren't intended to be used.'

These invitations began as a list of 'personal reminders', which were then transformed into type studies and packaged as a postcard set to send to other practitioners. She explains, 'It was an opportunity to try a few new things, including computational generation and in-camera letter construction.'

1 *You are cordially invited to . . . I wish*
2 *You are cordially invited to . . . make with wonder*

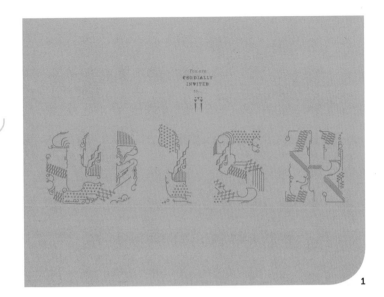

1

2

MATT LYON
London, UK

Where most lettering artists battle constantly with issues of legibility, Matt Lyon relishes the opportunity to make people think. He admits, 'At times I push things a little too far, but this is when I find design at its most exciting – when words and letters serve a wider function than just their legibility.'

Lyon's freehand drawings, sketched with fountain pens or brushes, are scanned and completely retraced in Illustrator to create vector outlines from which to work. The vivid colours and pattern-like textures, so characteristic of Lyon's work, are added in Photoshop.

All of the works shown here and on the next spread are self-initiated, some from his Daily Drawing project, others typographic experiments. The influence of folk-art patterning, decorative lettering and psychedelic lettering of the 1960s is obvious.

1

2

1 *Extra sensory perception*

2 *Memory eternal ripe*

3 *War. Peace. Heaven. Hell. Night. Day*
(a collection of verbal opposites)

4 *V*

THE NIGHT IS LONG THAT NEVER FINDS THE DAY

31 JUL 2011

5

7

5 *The night is long that never finds the day*

6 *What you are comes to you*

7 *This is the house that Jack built*

6

JAIME
VAN WART
Raleigh, North Carolina,
USA

Custom lettering forms a major component of Van Wart's work and many of his ideas evolve into full typefaces. He is drawn to the unique nature that lettering brings to a piece; the sense of warmth and personality that cannot always be achieved by using existing typefaces. Designing scripts and letters based on vintage signs and handwriting is what he particuarly loves. He begins all his ideas in a sketchbook, with a 0.5mm lead retractable pencil, followed by a 0.05mm black Micron, and then fills in with a brush pen. He then scans his drawings and refines them in Illustrator using a trackball mouse.

Van Wart enjoys looking through shelves of books, gathering images, taking notes and sketching formal details to learn as much as he can about certain styles, materials and the technical limitations of tools.

1

Bright young things with naked gods & holy liars (. . .)

KELLY THORN
Philadelphia, Pennsylvania, USA

This image is part of a poster series that was undertaken as a university project and done for the Rolling Road Show, a series of travelling movie screenings. Thorn's theme was road-trip movies, hence the map-like grid and roads forming the lettering.

Thorn says she has always found it difficult not to include words in her art, at first thinking it was a limitation but, recently, realising its strength. She especially loves the history of lettering. She explains, 'These days, people take for granted the countless hours that go into fonts, and forget the rich history that comes with letters.'

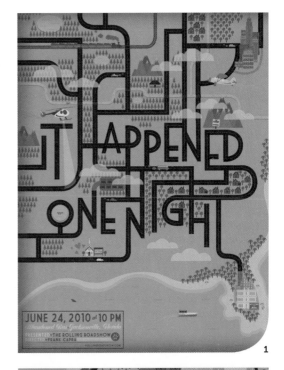

1 *It happened one night*
2 Detail

TOBY & PETE
Sydney, New South Wales, Australia

The main aim of the designers at Toby & Pete is to give life to the letters they are illustrating and to visually enhance the message behind the word. They do this by maintaining a very realistic element in their work. They visualise the letterforms in a three-dimensional space and treat them as if they are real and tangible objects. They picture how they would appear if they did actually exist, so they try not to have any intersecting letters or gravity-defying physics. The environment in which the type exists is always a product of the meaning behind the message.

The relaunch name cards shown on page 31 were developed to communicate the depth of the directorial team, now working as part of the collective that is Toby & Pete. They rebranded themselves with 10 different name combinations in the form of beautiful type treatments.

1

3

2

4

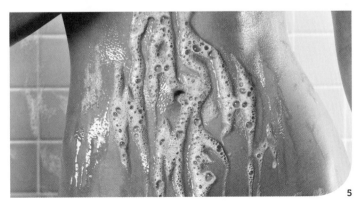

5

1 *Steve Back*

2 *Eva & Eddi*

3 *Anton & Jerry*

4 *Randy and Fez*

5 *Wash me*

LUKE LUCAS
Melbourne, Victoria, Australia

The custom lettering and typography of Luke Lucas is born out of the skate culture and graffiti of the 1980s, but it was not until he began *Lifelounge Magazine* that he began to experiment with font design, custom lettering and typographic illustration.

'I love that, based on the treatment and typographic style it receives, the same word can take on a variety of different meanings and evoke a whole spectrum of emotions,' says Lucas.

Just My Type was created for the Go Font Ur Self exhibition series and was inspired by classical Spencerian-style script, although the letterforms and ligatures are completely custom. No 3D software was used: the lettering has been given a three-dimensional appearance through the displacement of the pattern.

1

1 *Just my type*

MATS OTTDAL
Oslo, Norway

Mats Ottdal works on design projects within typography, illustration, branding and packaging design, but his biggest passion is typography. This began when he was a child, when he was inspired by movie posters and CD covers with great lettering. He believes type is the best way to express and communicate something and that it can also be the most enjoyable way to do so.

Ottdal starts by drawing ideas in his sketchbook before doing any work on the computer. While Adobe Illustrator is his program of choice, he finds it can sometimes ruin a good idea. There is always the danger you can 'overdesign' the early stages of a type project when not restricted to paper and pen, so he always enjoys going back to the sketchbook and starting over again.

1

1 *Antistress. The big day out. Bergen. Oslo. Violent afterparty (. . .)*

DADO QUEIROZ
Amsterdam, the Netherlands

Although often appearing to be three-dimensional, the lettering works of Dado Queiroz are, in fact, created entirely on the computer – from his very early composition roughs through to the elaborately shaded final pieces.

He begins each project by looking for a link between the letterforms, some form of harmony, to create a prototype. Then, using his most trusted tool, an Intuos3 medium-sized tablet, he is able to digitally draw into Photoshop with the brush and eraser tools, in much the same way as others would sketch on paper.

He will sometimes, although not in the case of any of the examples shown here, create vector line work to outline the letters, and work from those. The final part of his process involves the shading, which is done either manually or using effects within Photoshop or Illustrator.

1

2

3

5

4

1 *Ideafixa presents lettering workshop:*
LWC (. . .)
2 *Immersion*
3 *Ideafixa presents lettering workshop*
with Dado Queiroz (. . .)
4 *Fear is for girls*
5 *Yeah!*

ILOVEDUST
Southsea / London, UK

All the work produced at ilovedust results from a highly collaborative process that begins with a group brainstorm and an introduction of the basic concepts involved in a project. From these discussions, specific ideas are developed and explored, both on paper and on screen. Preliminary sketches are generally hand drawn with pen and ink and then worked on in Illustrator and Photoshop using a Wacom tablet. If an extra three-dimensional quality is needed, the final piece is finished in Cinema 4D.

The animal alphabet opposite was an internal project that the ilovedust team undertook in order to play with illustration within typography.

1

2

1 Detail
2 *T / t tiger shark. X / x xenopus. Z / z zeren. Y / y yak (...)*

JOEY CAMACHO
Los Angeles, California, USA

This series, inspired by a break-up, was created for those who look for simple inspiration in times of need. The message is a reminder to focus on the simple things in life, like love, laughter, learning and living.

Camacho first started working with type at university. He says, 'I was moved by the impact of pairing strong typographical style with inspirational concepts and meaningful messages.'

His design process begins with words, phrases and ideas jotted down in a notebook, which are then translated into Illustrator vectors. They are next worked on in Cinema 4D and, finally, in Photoshop for the textural work. With three-dimensional renders, the key is quality lighting and composition.

1 *Love better*
2 *Live stronger*

1

2

JOHN PASSAFIUME
Brooklyn, New York, USA

John Passafiume is Senior Designer at Louise Fili Ltd, a boutique firm with an emphasis on lettering design. Here he has completed many varied projects, including the cover design for Louise Filli and Steven Heller's lettering compendium, *Scripts*. Designed to complement the book's content, the lettering references scripts from the late nineteenth to the early twentieth century.

Passafiume speaks of the demanding process of hand lettering and the amount of energy it takes to craft such letterforms, explaining that 'lettering would have more in common with carpentry and print making than graphic design as such'.

The letter N, also shown on this page, was submitted as part of Jessica Hische's (see pages 16–19) Daily Drop Cap project. It draws on historical French hand lettering.

Passafiume's hand-drawn work can be seen on pages 126–127.

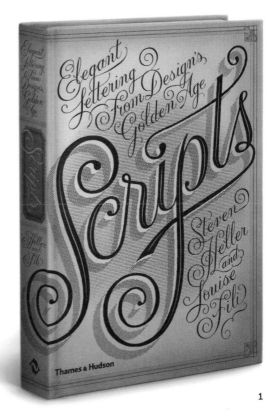

1

2

1 *Elegant lettering from design's golden age.*
Scripts. Steven Heller and Louise Fili
2 *N*

SEAN FREEMAN
London, UK

'I like the power of words . . . and my passion is really bringing them to life.'

Although Sean Freeman admits to spending a great deal of time working in Photoshop, his initial groundwork is often very much hands-on, and the spectrum of materials he uses is huge. Photographing elements of the materials and then composing them in Photoshop allows him to create textural and dynamic results. For the work shown on this page, for example, he photographed ribbon in the form of lettering.

It is the accessibility of lettering that draws Freeman – the fact that, through illustrating letters, everyone will understand the work. Often his ideas will evolve from the textures he uses, and these materials, more often than not, will enhance the written words.

1

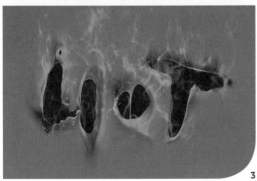

1 *All you need is love*
2 *Illustration*
3 *Hot*

4

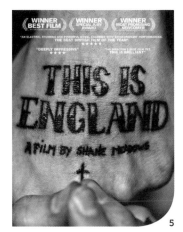

4 *Band of horses*
5 *This is England, a film by Shane Meadows*
6 *Fear*
7 *The Decemberists*

STEVEN BONNER
Stirling, UK

Steven Bonner believes lettering is very similar to illustration. 'The letters are my characters and, as long as I keep the communicative aspects intact, I can apply any style I like to them. The style of the lettering often says more than the words themselves,' he explains.

He starts a piece with rough sketches, but avoids too much detail so as not to lose the 'flow' of the process. He then uses Adobe Creative Suite, and a Wacom Intuos3 A5 Wide tablet and pen to transform his ideas digitally. He says, 'I like the clean look vectors give me, and it suits my aesthetic.'

The penguin letter A was created for the cover of *The Art Book*. He was asked to recreate the process he used for this for a magazine tutorial, which resulted in the swan letter *S*.

1

3

4

1 *S*

2 *a*

3 *For designers every day
not everyday designers*

2   4 *The art of type*

JIM DATZ
Brooklyn, New York, USA

Jim Datz always begins his lettering work with what he terms 'doodles', revising them over and over by hand before even thinking of translating them digitally.

Shown here is a series of drop caps Datz was commissioned to design by *Fortune* magazine. The theme was to create fashion-oriented letters, which gave him the opportunity to incorporate some playful illustration along with the letterforms themselves.

More examples of Datz's hand lettering can be found on pages 104–105.

1 Various capital letters

1

SIMON ÅLANDER
Karlskrona, Sweden

Although a student of digital media, Simon Ålander relishes opportunities to mix analogue and digital methods to create custom typography. He creates lettering both for branding and for his own personal projects. Hugely inspired by music, many of his works quote directly from songs or their titles.

When describing the strength of his approach, Ålander says, 'I think subtle textures and shadings are my secret weapons for success.'

Ålander admits the greatest struggle is the combination of certain letters and attaining the perfect balance, flow and composition of a print. Sketching many draft versions before settling and digitising his work helps to overcome these challenges.

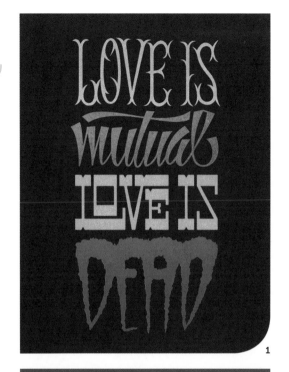

1

2

1 *Love is mutual. Love is dead*
2 *Horse Bay Blues*

JAMIE LAWSON
Hamilton, Ontario, Canada

Zoo was created by Jamie Lawson of Poly as the identity for an art exhibition. The aim was to show a kind of decadence to set the tone for the show. 'The spirit of the Zoo show was related to Victorian menageries and even older bestiaries – we wanted something evocative of that antique spirit while also reflecting the thoroughly modern sensibilities of the work being shown,' explains Lawson.

Lawson often uses existing fonts as a basis from which to create his designs. He sees them as being like the scaffolding of a building in that, more often than not, the final piece is so far removed from the original font that it's impossible to deduce what the original font is. He pays great attention to how the forms relate to each other and the composition as a whole.

For examples of Lawson's hand-generated work, see pages 148–149.

1

1 *Zoo or a motley menagerie of magnificent mammalia*

SKYRILL
Manama, Bahrain

The designers at Skyrill explore new possibilities of mixing media in typography, with special attention paid to how the whole set of letters looks together as one collection.

For the Type Fluid Experiment, they collected images of water splashes, paint splashes – different forms of fluids and liquids reacting to various things – to provide the reference for capturing the shape, colour, friction and other characteristics of liquids. They used the programs RealFlow and 3D Studio Max to create the renderings of each individual letter.

'Typography is usually about sticking to the grid and keeping every side and angle calculated. This experiment broke the rules and came up with something new,' says Hussain Almossawi. Plans to create three-dimensional models of the letterforms are in the pipeline.

1

2

3

1 *abc*

2 *s*

3 *v*

PEOPLE COLLECTIVE

Melbourne, Victoria, Australia

Aaron Moodie and Colin Trechter are People Collective. They revel in creating work that has a strong conceptual grounding and are most happy when type and working by hand overlap. They approach every project by first brainstorming on their own and then coming together to compare resolutions and go on from there.

Shown here is some of the diverse lettering work they have created for the literary magazine *Voiceworks*. This being a magazine that features writing, photography and illustrations, there was plenty of scope to play with customised typography, especially on the covers.

Describing their approach, Trechter says, 'We lean towards illustrative typographic covers. Generally we are looking for a certain level of play and meaning, so that the covers function and can be read on numerous levels.'

1

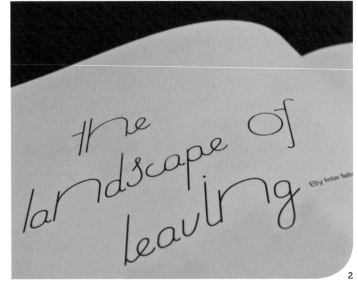

2

3

1 *The masquerade party*

2 *The landscape of leaving*

3 *Voiceworks* magazine, assorted covers

MARIAN BANTJES

Bowen Island, British Columbia, Canada

Marian Bantjes spent 15 months writing, illustrating and designing *I Wonder*; every page features type and image in an integrated way. The elaborate pattern on the cover ties in with the lettering, with gold and silver foils and gilded page edges providing an added luxury.

Although she begins with pen and paper, she does very little by hand. Instead she will meticulously trace in Illustrator from the original, resulting in the detail of the vector art for which she is well known.

It is very important to Bantjes that her work be both structured and intriguing. She wants people to spend time looking at it and has the grand aim of bringing delight to the viewer.

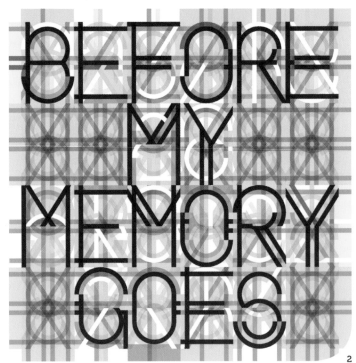

1 *I wonder*

2 *Before my memory goes*

TOM LANE
Bristol, UK

This book cover shows the highly intricate and extravagant style that has become typical of Tom Lane's lettering work (see also page 129). The design for Heston Blumenthal's cookery book was heavily inspired by the Book of Kells (an illuminated manuscript of the Celtic monks).

Lane begins with pencil or Japanese brush-and-ink drawings, which he then refines with the aid of a light box before translating them into Illustrator via his Wacom tablet. This process of hand generation is very important in his projects. He says, 'The act of drawing really nice curves, moving from thick and thin forms, inking up sketches so you can see the fruit of your labours, is just bliss to me.'

1

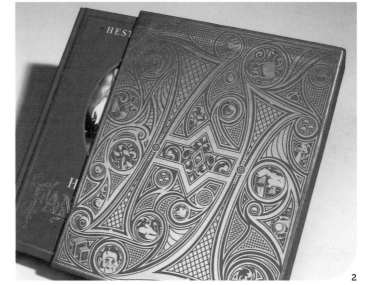

2

1 *B*
2 *H*

JON CONTINO
Brooklyn, New York, USA

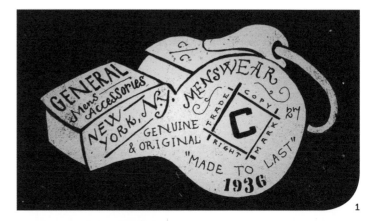

In Contino's words, 'Most of my work is rooted in Americana-based signage. I like to tell a story of environment and age in my lettering and illustration work. It is all based on meticulously researched details.'

His work is all hand drawn initially and is then digitised once finalised. Contino reveals his secret for emulating the deterioration of signage as 'playing with wet ink, scanning at different resolutions and using the Levels palette in Photoshop'.

The example on the opposite page was created for CXXVI Clothing Co., of which Contino is both co-founder and Creative Director. Influenced by early 1900s garment tags and the notion of American product pride, this example emulates these themes in a very tongue-in-cheek way.

1 *Menswear. 'Made to last' (. . .)*
2 *Maps that changed the world*
3 *Seal of quality.*
'A gentleman's brand' (. . .)

3

LINZIE HUNTER

London, UK

'I tend to approach lettering from the perspective of an illustrator rather than a typographer. I see each letter as an individual illustration that combines to create a finished image.'

Linzie Hunter's lettering work is designed to be both functional and decorative, and she uses the type in many instances to add pattern and texture to a composition.

Beginning with colour sketches, Hunter will most often then use a Wacom pen and tablet, working straight into Photoshop or Illustrator. Colour is of great importance and is a big part of the development stage of her work.

1

1 *Comma. Ellipsis. Space. Apostrophe. Interrobang (. . .)*

2 *Obtain. Attribute. Distribute.*

Distinct. Perspective. Acquire. (. . .)

2

3 *Green. Recycle. Earth. Organic (. . .)*

McFADDEN & THORPE
San Francisco, California, USA

The work of Brett McFadden and Scott Thorpe is deeply rooted in typographic exploration. This is usually the starting point of a project and, often, type will be drawn specifically for a project.

'We love the way the forms of letters create a secondary language that piggybacks the primary message contained in the text. A letterform can express any range of emotions, or at times, the absence of emotion,' says McFadden.

Most of their lettering is completed on the computer, so much of the exploration happens in trying to translate the concept to the screen.

The Mission Arts poster shown here was designed from the outset to be optimised when screenprinted. The letterforms are made up of two colours, which, when overprinted with the ink, create a third colour and all lock together perfectly.

1 *Presenting the 2010 Mission Arts Trail Guide. Excellent!*
2 *Our lines are open*

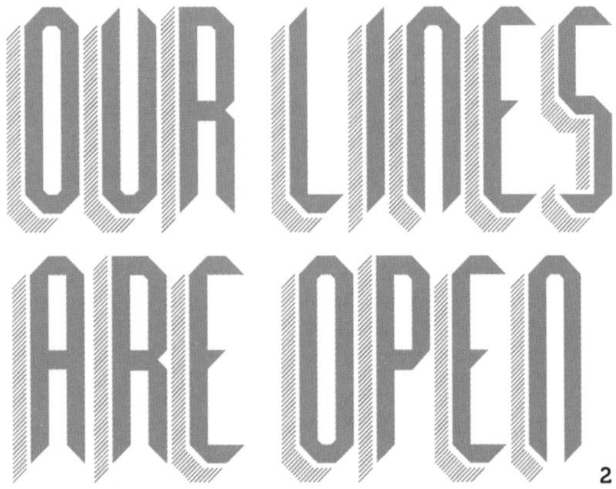

DREW MELTON
Grand Rapids, Michigan, USA

All the works shown here are part of Melton's online community, 'The Phraseology project', a group involved in the exploration of typography. The final artwork for his lettering pieces is digitally created, but he always begins by mind-mapping and loosely sketching thoughts. He then looks for typefaces or illustration styles that fit the mood.

Aside from receiving a very basic introduction to typography in college, Melton is completely self-taught, but he has always enjoyed the power of communication and language, especially the range of expression possible inside 26 characters.

To complete Nothing Worth Doing Is Easy, Melton spent the day in an old antiques shop looking for original inspiration. He says, 'I came across some old certificates. They were absolutely beautiful documents with some of the best lettering work I have ever seen. I wanted to work on something with that level of detail. This comes nowhere close to the pieces I found.'

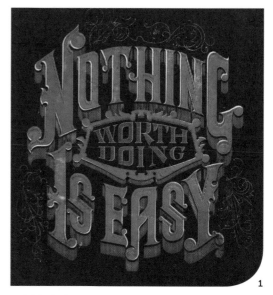

1

2

1 *Nothing worth doing is easy*
2 *Once upon a time. . .*

ALONZO FELIX
Brooklyn, New York, USA

The letters featured here were all created as part of the Lettercult website's Alphabattle – a fortnightly project to create custom letterforms for each letter of the alphabet. Dollar bills, Austrian heritage and Victorian flourishes are some of the influences that were drawn upon.

Alonzo Felix, a design student, calls lettering his 'full-time obsession'. He draws on his knowledge of typographic history and is influenced by masters of the craft, such as Herb Lubalin, as well as the lettering found in vintage advertising. To Felix, lettering 'offers an invitation into the beauty of the words we all read every day'.

1

2

3

1 *A*
2 *B*
3 *Q*

SEB LESTER
London, UK

Shown here are a number of limited-edition art prints created by Seb Lester. His expressive and dramatic lettering, as well as the use of metallic inks and alternative printing methods, make these works precious and collectible pieces of art.

Lester believes that 'The best lettering, like the best calligraphy, is about controlled freedom.'

Lester's lettering methods are rooted in calligraphy, but it's also clear to see the influence of medieval illumination and ornamentation running through his work. The result is a timeless style that could just as easily be inscribed in stone as placed on a gallery wall.

The Shimmering Beauty, a print that came about after 'hundreds of sketches and scribbles', is designed as an ambigram. That is, it reads both ways up.

1

3

2

1 *We shape our destiny if we believe in the beauty of our dreams*
2 *The shimmering beauty of heaven in blazing sunshine*
3 *The shimmering beauty of sunshine blazing in heaven*

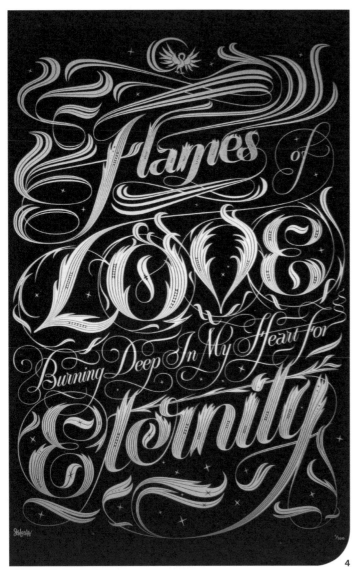

4 *Flames of love burning deep in my heart for eternity*

5 *I know nothing with any certainty, but the sight of the stars makes me dream. Van Gogh*

6 *TITS 1, Great tit. 2, Blue tit. 3,. Crested tit. 4, Marsh-tit*

MICHAL SYCZ
Warsaw, Poland

Michal Sycz mostly uses 3D programs but has also tried combining three-dimensional letters with studio shots, photo manipulations and vectors. He believes that an open mind and creativity are the keys to success.

Sycz feels that 'Lettering is an art form in itself. I love how each typeface has individual things that make it different. It can be beautiful and communicative.'

Each piece is begun with a quick low-resolution sketch. The next step is to create a vector draft, then three-dimensional renders or studio shots.

I Kill You was created for Poland Art Group and, with that title as his starting theme, Sycz decided to create typographic artwork using cigarettes. He used his own handwriting as the basis for the font, then added some three-dimensional tricks to achieve the final artwork.

1 *I kill you, smoking kills, lose, win (. . .)*

1

ED NACIONAL
Brooklyn, New York, USA

Ed Nacional uses geometric shapes and limited palettes of bold colours. In developing his lettering, he will often reference existing fonts or vintage type examples or, alternatively, he will layer two overlapping shapes or colours.

The use of texture is also an important part of Nacional's work. Hello Friend, one of a number of pieces shown here that was created for the Friends of Type website, uses an old photocopier scan for its texture.

High Lite & Low Down was inspired by highlighters and pencils, which were used to create the thicks and thins of the letterforms, whereas Under the Weather is composed of lines of raindrops. Nacional explains, 'You can choose typefaces that will fit your design, but when you use custom lettering, it makes for a much more cohesive piece.'

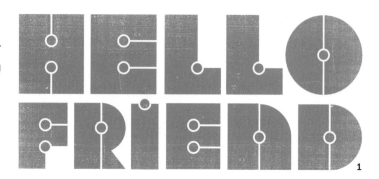

1

2

3

4

5

1 *Hello friend*
2 *High lite &*
low down
3 *Under the*
weather
4 *You, me &*
the sea
5 *Higher fives*

ANDRÉ BEATO

London, UK

Portuguese designer and illustrator André Beato describes lettering as being like a 'kind of game' in that the final result needs to be both legible and attractive. Of his technique secrets he reveals, 'I use some glows, gradient shadow techniques and some textures at times to add personality and style to the final work.'

The Life Aquatic was a personal project. Beato felt that the branding for the comedy film of the same name, by Wes Anderson, could have been handled better, so he came up with the idea of using the red hats of Team Zissou (the crew members of the sea vessel featured in the film) and created an embroidered type to fit.

1 *Support Japan*
2 *Honor and pride*
3 *The life aquatic*
4 *Naughty amour*

1

The lettering reads:

SALVATION ARMY
One hundred years of service

BROOKLYN KDU X IDN HONG KONG

HONOR AND PRIDE

THE KEYSTONE DESIGN UNION
DIVISION OF GRAPHICAL MIND CONTROL | GLOBAL TALENT ARMY

2

THE LIFE AQUATIC

3

NAUGHTY L'AMOUR

4

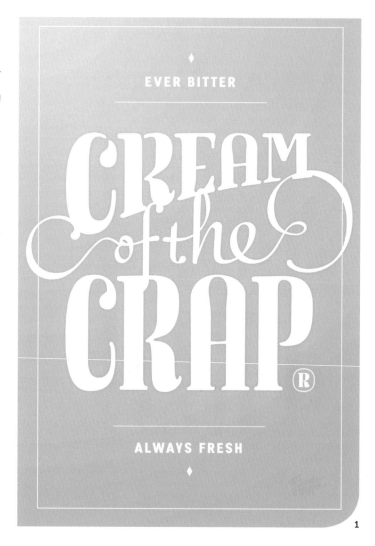

AARON CARÁMBULA

Brooklyn, New York, USA

'Lettering is for me a natural extension of [type and typography] – part of the full spectrum of language made visible.'

A core member of Friends of Type, an online collective, Aaron Carámbula is drawn to the way in which lettering can use visual tools to create powerful language. Although most comfortable working digitally, he is constantly experimenting and pushing his own comfort zone. He shifts from computer to pencil sketches several times before coming up with the refined final image.

Cream of the Crap, featured here, is influenced by vintage American milk bottles. However, so as to limit the risk of following any style too closely, Carámbula avoided looking at any actual examples.

1 *Cream of the crap.*
Ever bitter. Always fresh

DAN CASSARO
Brooklyn, New York, USA

Dan Cassaro is especially fond of the way lettering can recontextualise words and enhance the meaning of whatever information is being communicated.

Cassaro feels that it is difficult to achieve work that demonstrates the human touch. He says, 'I'm constantly striving to make things imperfect in just the right way . . . Anyone can do the math, but I'm more interested in eliciting a more human response.'

The alphabet shown here was commissioned for MTV Networks for use on one of their award shows. The letters are modelled on the basic shapes of Helvetica with an added dimension creating the illusion of folded paper or tape.

1

2

1 *Open highway reader*

2 Alphabet

RICHARD PEREZ
San Francisco, California, USA

Richard Perez started his company, Skinny Ships, as a way of exploring new design and illustration techniques beyond those that his studies allowed him to. He now creates lettering for self-gratification and for commissions and collaborations.

Perez describes his attraction to lettering as the desire to take a universal form and find a new way to look at it. He explains, 'I'm always interested in twisting simple shapes into unique lettering forms.'

Perez says he has about three or four boxes of textures that he uses to scan in and apply to his digital lettering work. This aspect, as well as his use of clear geometric forms and bright colour combinations, gives his work a character beyond simply computerised vector art.

1 *Blah! Blah! Blah! Blah!*
2 *Hello friends*

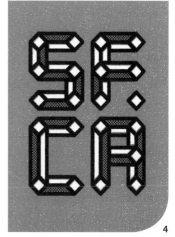

3 *Keep on exploring*

4 *SF. CA*

5 *Staying busy*

CRAIG&KARL

New York, New York,
USA / Sydney, New
South Wales, Australia

Despite living on different sides of the world, Craig Redman and Karl Maier still manage to collaborate on a daily basis to create an array of playful and bold lettering and illustrative design work. They confess their secret to digital lettering as being the 'snap to grid' function – ensuring all lettering aligns and sits together in perfect harmony.

Redman and Maier begin either by sketching out ideas or by simply drawing straight into Freehand on the computer. Shown here is an array of their work, both commissioned and self-initiated projects. Experimenting with liquid forms and candy stripes, dry paintbrush effects and sewing thread are just some examples of their influences.

1

3

2

4

1 *Twas a dark and stormy night*
2 *'I think he might have eaten way too many Argentinian empanadas.'*
3 *The house of love*
4 *High and dry*

Chapter 2:
Hand-drawn and Illustrated Lettering

Contemporary letterers attempt to go beyond technology to create something fresh. For many, the joy of crafting something with their hands, and using traditional tools to do so, is what entices them to work in this way.

There are many techniques and tools that can be used to create hand-lettered compositions, and each artist and designer showcased in this chapter has developed his or her own methods, tricks and combinations. The choices they make and the skills they have developed are, for the most part, the result of careful (and plentiful) experimentation in drawing and tracing letterforms.

The initial – and probably the most vital – stage of using hand-drawn lettering for a piece of work is planning the overall composition. Unlike working on a computer, with paper you don't have the option of simply clicking a button to change the colour of a word or increase the size of a letter. Careful sketching and planning are key to ensure that a design does not have to be redrawn in full over and over again. Some letterers will develop a substantial pile of rough sketches to plot both the spacing of the letters and the styling of the type accurately before beginning to work on their final piece. Tracing paper (or layout paper) is often used at this stage to progressively refine the visuals by a process of drawing, tracing and amending.

2

For the letterforms themselves, practitioners either create them from scratch or draw influence from existing fonts. Becoming accustomed to the forms of letters through tracing existing ones is a great way of capturing the curves and peculiarities of each letter. Many practitioners use this as the basis for their working process.

The final stages may include using pen or ink, or a combination of media, as a permanent piece of work begins to take shape. Texture and accuracy are key in these stages and, as colour is added, a final piece of work is created. Completed lettering is often scanned into the computer and tidied up to prepare it for digital output.

1 Tracing paper is a useful material for making slight variations to sketches, as shown here in the work of Jim Tierney (see pages 102–103)
2 Letitia Buchan (see page 121), shown here in her work space, uses a range of pens in varying thicknesses to create her free-flowing letterforms

3 The assortment of materials Esther Aarts (see page 89) uses to create her lettering 'doodles'

TOOLS

Pencil

Use of a medium-weight pencil is vital in drawing letterforms, both to reduce the ugly and messy smudging that soft pencils create and to ensure the lines are still easy to erase and alter. A soft pencil is a popular choice; alternatively, a mechanical pencil dispenses with the need for a sharpener.

Eraser

A kneaded eraser (putty eraser) is a good option as it can be moulded to suit the needs of working on both large areas and very fine points. In addition, it won't leave graphite marks on the work.

Correction fluid

This can be useful if you prefer using pen or ink for rough sketches, as it allows small mistakes to be touched up.

Tracing paper

Tracing paper is very useful during the planning stages of lettering work – laying one sheet over another will allow you to repeat letterforms until perfect.

Ink

Drawing ink, usually water-soluble, is a popular medium as its steady flow leaves letters streak-free.

Brushes

Although brushes can be difficult to master, when used with ink and a steady hand, they can produce fluid and elegant strokes. The hairs on the ends of some lettering brushes are set flat to allow for making precise edges.

Pens

A letterer will often use a range of fine-line pens for outlining letters and intricate elements. Rollerball fountain pens are also a popular choice due to the wide range of interchangeable nib shapes and sizes.

Marker pens

These come in a range of thicknesses and shapes and can provide a fast and streak-free means of blocking in large areas of colour. Chisel tips are useful for hard edges, while wider, rounded markers are good for filling in.

DANA TANAMACHI

Brooklyn, New York, USA

Dana Tanamachi specialises in large chalk installations. The beauty of lettering in chalk is that she can easily start again if something doesn't look right. On this point she says, 'I am constantly erasing, redrawing and erasing some more until I get it exactly the way I want it.'

She begins all her designs by researching visual archives before making sketches, which she then scans into the computer and inverts to give the effect of a blackboard. With this done, she draws her compositions onto the walls. On occasion, for more lasting installations, such as the Free Admission To Those Who Dream piece shown here, she will finish the piece off with permanent chalk pens. The blue poster was drawn in chalk on blue-coloured blackboard paint, with no Photoshop editing whatsoever done to the final piece.

1

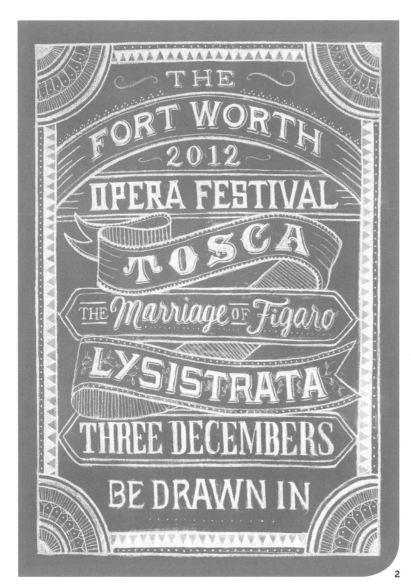

3

4

1 *New York. Free admission to those who dream. Matinee at 3. Twice nightly*
2 *The Fort Worth 2012 Opera Festival. Tosca. The Marriage of Figaro. Lysistrata. Three Decembers. Be drawn in*
3 *The Wes Anderson Brooklyn*
4 Detail

2

MARY KATE McDEVITT

Portland, Oregon, USA

It is the nostalgic quality of lettering that Mary Kate McDevitt is drawn to – not just the nod to vintage typography, but also the skill of hand-drawn letterforms. She explains, 'Once I learnt cursive, it was non-stop decorations all over my notebooks, then I worked on bubble letters, then punk-rock letters and now I draw letters for people.'

This selection of work, created to sell through her online shop, primarily comprises hand-printed posters, cards and hand-painted blackboards. All her projects begin with rough pencil sketches, then research. She says 'I reference a lot of vintage-type work when I feel stuck for composition or styling ideas.' From here, either using a fountain pen or one-shot lettering paint (if the design is destined for her blackboards), she adds weight, texture and detail to the line work to create the final piece.

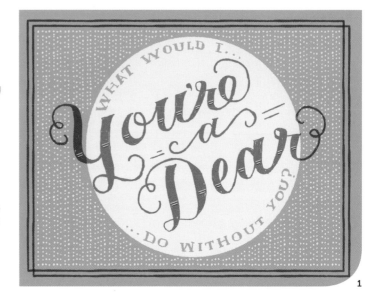

1

2

1 *You're a dear. What would I do without you?*

2 *Aren't handwritten letters ace?*

3 *After coffee I will . . . much better! Feels good to get some stuff done! Write it. Do it. Erase it*

4 *High 5*

5 *Fresh and delicious 100%*

6 *Write more hand-written letters*
7 *Consistency is the last refuge of the unimaginative. Oscar Wilde*

ERIK MARINOVICH

San Francisco,
California, USA

Erik Marinovich is an illustrator, designer and co-founder of the online type and lettering collective Friends of Type, along with three friends (see pages 14, 15, 70). Together they create work for their sketchblog and collaborate on client projects while always following the motto 'Make it for the book'.

He explains that 'Crafting letterforms uses many techniques and processes that allow for an infinite number of possibilities. It just never gets old and there is always something new to discover in a letterform.'

His work explores a range of media from hand-generated to digital to three-dimensional (see page 162), depending on what best suits the project. This hand-drawn piece was rendered in ink on paper before being scanned, then coloured in Photoshop.

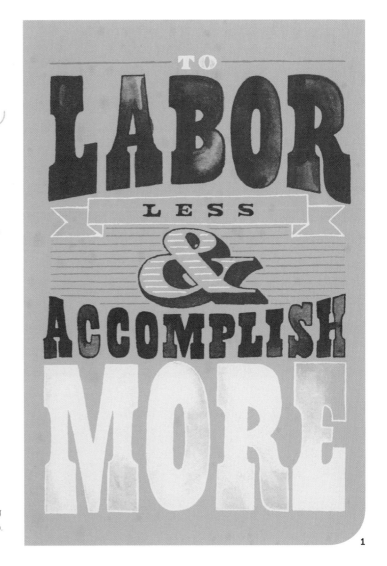

1

1 *To labor less & accomplish more*

JEFF ROGERS
Astoria, New York, USA

'People really respond and connect to words. As an image maker, I love to combine a certain aesthetic with letterforms and create a look that works with what the words are saying.'

Jeff Rogers uses a combination of hand-drawn and digital techniques, his process varying with every project. He almost always begins with pencil sketches and then often moves on to Illustrator (to make vector outlines) and Photoshop (to add texture and colour). Sometimes, in the case of hand-finished works, he will use the digital work as the guide for the painting.

In many cases, he merges his love of painting with his more recent discovery of lettering. The mural shown here was commissioned for the Ace Hotel in New York and takes a lyric from a Prince song as inspiration. He projected the scanned letterforms onto the canvas before painstakingly applying paint.

1

2

1 *You can dance if you want to. All the critics love you in New York*
2 Detail
3 *Her friends forgot their drunken promises*
4 *Shoes shoes shoes for me & for yous*

ANDY SMITH

Hastings,
East Sussex, UK

Andy Smith combines illustration and typography with an optimistic, humorous twist. Smith's background is screenprinting, and he aims to carry this aesthetic through to his lettering work, despite it being digitally printed in most cases.

'I'll lay out the type in Helvetica on the computer, then sketch it out and think about fonts. I have lots of font-reference books that I can look at,' Smith explains. 'Then I'll start drawing the type in ink, then scan it and assemble it in Photoshop. I work in layers so that I can keep a screenprinted feel by just using a few colours and letting them overlap.'

All of the examples shown here were completed using these methods. Not For The Likes Of You is a personal project designed for an exhibition of alternative royal wedding invitations.

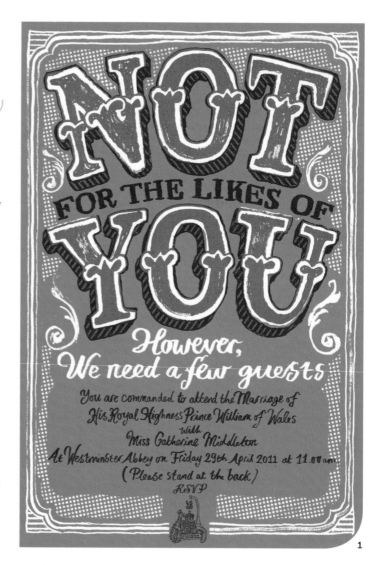

1

1 *Not for the likes of you. However, we need a few guests (. . .)*

ESTHER AARTS
Nijmegen,
the Netherlands

The lettering style of Esther Aarts is full of fun. While she has no lack of commissioned projects, she fuels her love of lettering by constantly drawing and completing personal projects.

To Aarts 'Letters are characters, literally. They all have their own characteristics. I enjoy how the boundaries of designing text are wide enough to experiment and be playful but also provide me with a set of rules to keep me on track.'

She used 'cheapish, foul-smelling black markers and white correction fluid' to create the black-and-white 'marker doodle' shown on this page. These may go on to form the basis for more elaborate colour lettering, to test out combinations of characters and forms.

1

2

1 *Knock on wood*

2 *Xmas controller (. . .)*

CARSON ELLIS
Portland, Oregon, USA

Ever since receiving a calligraphy kit as a child, Carson Ellis has been drawing letters both for pleasure and work. Mainly an illustrator of children's books, she also works with bands, in particular The Decemberists, for whom she has completed much promotional material. The posters shown here were hand-illustrated with either pen, pencil, nib pen or gouache, and then screenprinted.

To describe her process, Ellis says, 'I'm a meticulous sketcher so I only tend to make one. I'll spend a lot of time on it, then I'll paint and ink it.'

Ellis spends time researching font references before designing her letterforms. While she is personally drawn to the more elaborate and ornate letterforms, her detailed illustrations usually require a simplified style.

1

2

1 *Tumble bee. Laura Veirs sings folk songs for children*

2 *Special delivery. Danger! Fragile (. . .)*

3 / 4 *The Decemberists (. . .)*

5 *Salutations*

SASHA PROOD
Brooklyn, New York, USA

Themes in Sasha Prood's work usually tend towards the organic and the scientific. The influence of nature is evident through the use of earthy colour palettes as well as the choices of subject matter. A variety of animals and plants are commonly found entwined in her letterforms.

For Prood, 'Lettering is the bridge between my classical training in graphic design and my passion for fine art. I love to merge imagery and typography, creating unexpected custom display type.' Most of the designs here were comissioned for magazines or other publications; all are entirely hand-drawn using either pencil or pen. Prood based the 'Manimals' letterforms on *Maxim* magazine's title font and introduced the humour of the article through the animals (the article was about people who have animal-like abilities or appearance).

1

2

1 *Manimals*
2 *Wired*
3 3 *Coming this summer*

LIAM STEVENS
London, UK

The use of hand-generated techniques and simple materials is very important to Liam Stevens. Not only do they give him a break from computers, they also allow him to be expressive. Working with a mechanical pencil for the most part, his work is very much about mark making and has almost a folk-art quality to it.

Stevens is influenced by old engraved type and borders. He created the alphabet for Anya Takes to the Thames as an experiment, and admits to having drafted many more in the hope of one day being able to finalise them as fonts.

Stevens works to a large scale when creating his type. He explains, 'This allows me to put in the details I want and shrink it down to suit the project.' For example, for the Anya Takes to the Thames invitations, the lettering was so large it spanned four A3 (297 × 420mm / 11¾ × 16½in) sheets before being shrunk down.

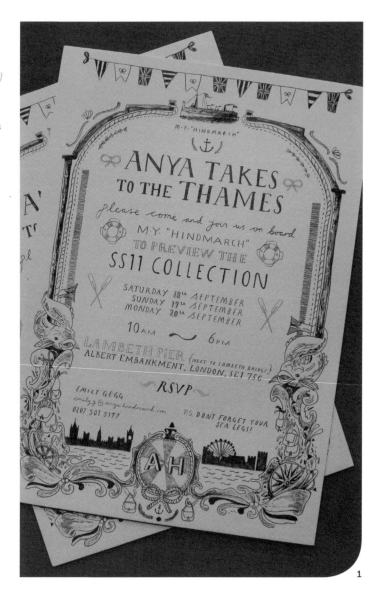

1

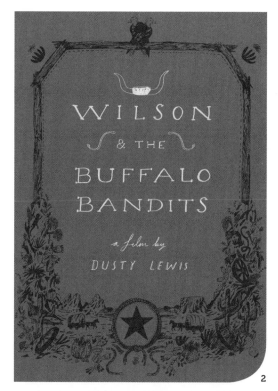

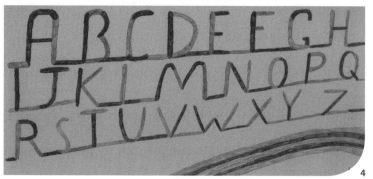

1 *Anya takes to the Thames (. . .)*
2 *Wilson & the Buffalo Bandits.*
A film by Dusty Lewis
3 *Pop Forest. New album.*
Secret Forces. Out now!
4 Alphabet

SARAH KING

Vancouver, British
Columbia, Canada

'I love the opportunity to hide stories in illustrations, using the letterforms as images and shapes to create textures.' Using as little computer editing as possible, Sarah King constructs images from her hand-sketched letterforms in much the same way a painter would shade with gradients of colour. Her lettering is an integral part of the composition and often provides all of the shapes used to construct the image.

Shown here is a selection of her work including two plates created for an exhibition. She drew them out first before applying them to ceramic transfer paper and firing them. One is representative of water while the other is inspired by space and the stars. Both themes are implied solely through the shapes, colours and angles of the letters, with no other line work at all.

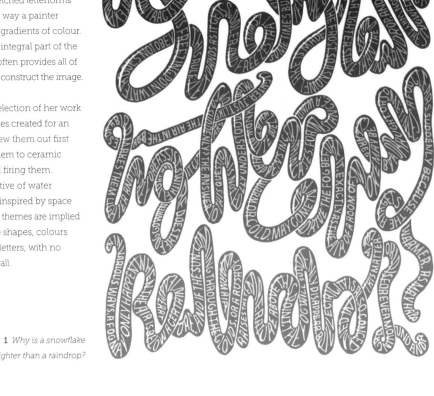

1 *Why is a snowflake
lighter than a raindrop?*

1

96 |

2

3

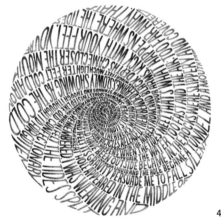

4

2 *Ever thought that such conspicuous markings as those of the zebra would (...)*
3 *Black stars. Space. Dish 250. Astronomers*
4 *What happens when the tides meet. That's what happens where the tides (...)*

NATE WILLIAMS
Los Angeles, California, USA

'I like to think of a letter as a puzzle. There is always a new way to draw a letter and the puzzle is figuring that out.'

Nate Williams loves the freedom of hand lettering, as it can create a tone and a mood unto itself. He likens it to the music in a horror movie. 'If you didn't have the creepy music when someone walked into the basement, it wouldn't be scary,' he says.

The brainstorming process in all of Williams' work is of the highest priority and is very extensive. He begins with word associations for imagery and lettering and then follows by quickly sketching ideas until the meaning has been communicated effectively. The final composition is often completed on the computer from a combination of scanned images.

1

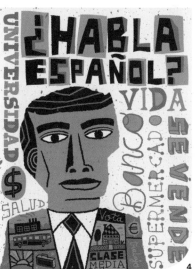

1 *He who plants a tree plants hope. Lucy Larcom*

2 *All Together Now. Beatles. Stuff for kids of all ages (. . .)*

3 *Sierra: Explore, enjoy and protect the planet. 10 coolest schools (. . .)*

4 *Do you speak Spanish? Life (. . .)*

ANDREW JOYCE
Bath, UK

Shown here are Andrew Joyce's illustrated letters – a personal project exploring the many forms of each letter of the alphabet. When developing this project, he kept his sketchbook with him at all times, adding new ideas and shapes as they came to him. The result is a reference catalogue of hand-drawn styles that he can use for future projects. He secretly admits that most of the colour combinations are taken from the NBA team logos.

To explain the appeal of lettering Joyce says, 'I really like the roughness to the work and the fact that you are able create something without necessarily being held back by too many rules or grids.' It is the mistakes and the imperfections of the lettering that make it so appealing to him as an art form.

1

1 Alphabet

TIMBA SMITS
London, UK

The examples of Timba Smits' work shown here
were created for his quarterly magazine, *Wooden Toy*.
Most of his work is done entirely by hand using pencils,
pens, markers, paint and the odd bit of coffee or tea bags
for texturing. On occasion, he will add textures digitally
from scans of old paper and other ephemera.

The secret to Smits' work is time. An alphabet he
created for one edition of the magazine took over
60 hours to complete.

French music producer Wax Tailor was the influence
for the House of Wax quarterly cover. Working from
a still image of a dripping candle, Smit created the type
to reflect the nature of wax as well as old 1970s and 1980s
horror-movie titles.

1 *The house of wax*
2 *Limited edition Wooden Toy*
   colab series (. . .)

JIM TIERNEY
Brooklyn, New York, USA

Jim Tierney designs and illustrates a large number of book covers for Penguin Books. Inspiration for the jacket designs comes mostly from elements of the narrative, such as setting or era.

The combination of the type and illustration is of key importance in his designs and each adds relevance to the other. Tierney admits, 'I guess I feel that lettering makes my art more engaging, and gives it a context.'

Tierney always has a ready supply of tracing paper at hand as he uses this along with brushes, pens and markers. Once the basic composition is established, he will separate out each colour onto its own layer of tracing paper, scanning each drawing so colour can be added digitally. This process, in addition to being cheap and portable, allows changes to be made to individual elements relatively easily.

1

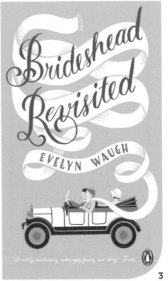

1 *This Is Just Exactly Like You.*
A novel by Drew Perry
2 *Jules Verne. Journey to the*
Center of the Earth
3 *Brideshead Revisited.*
Evelyn Waugh

JIM DATZ
Brooklyn, New York, USA

Initially working as a designer for corporate clients, Jim Datz (see also page 46) established his company, Neither Fish Nor Fowl, with the intention of fulfilling what he loves the most, which is 'making drawings of ideas that make people happy'. He now creates a range of illustrated goods, ranging from posters to T-shirts, and they almost always include lettering in some form.

Although he finishes his process by colouring and cleaning up on the computer, the vast majority of the lettering and illustration work is done by hand. This is very important to Datz as it enables the ideas to flow fast and fluidly and allows him to drift between his many ideas until the final piece shines through.

1

1 *Free the caged bird*

2 *Fancy a kebab?*

3 *Grow your own*

GRADY McFERRIN

Brooklyn, New York, USA

The desire to create something nostalgic and handmade, along with a deep respect for the age-old traditions of sign painting and calligraphy, are what inspire Grady McFerrin's lettering work. He says, 'Sometimes I spend hours looking through old books for the right lettering, sometimes I grab a Sharpie and just start lettering.'

Initially, McFerrin's process took more of a DIY approach of photocopying and distressing type, but now he uses other means – pen, pencil, brush and ink for example, along with the use of Photoshop for cleaning up and adding texture.

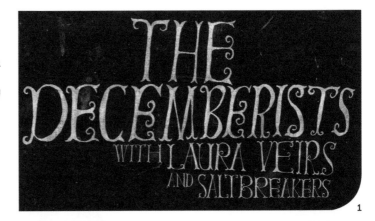

1 *The Decemberists with Laura Veirs and Saltbreakers*
2 *DPR Mass*

GEOFFREY HOLSTAD
Grand Rapids, Michigan, USA

'I rely on those moments where my lines stray from "perfect" to be uniquely mine.'

Geoffrey Holstad takes his inspiration from American folk art, and camp and farm signage. He explains 'I love hand signage made out of necessity; a strong, confident hand, never mind the wiggles, shakes and drips.' Shown here is one such sign for his online shop, Moosejaw Mountaineering, which he created using acrylic paint on board.

To carry this aesthetic through to his client lettering work, Holstad most often uses India ink on paper, relying on the computer as little as possible. This helps keep the natural feel of his work alive.

1

2

1 *Moosejaw Mountaineering*
2 *Grow some free food*

CHRISTOPHER SILAS NEAL

Brooklyn, New York, USA

Christopher Silas Neal is known for his strong illustration and lettering skills, which are employed for book jackets, posters, advertisements and packaging. He speaks of lettering as having 'the ability to make something feel one-of-a-kind and often from a different era'. He explains of his work, 'My letters are far less than perfect, and it's in those imperfect details that a design or image really comes to life.'

Neal uses pencil along with gouache and brush markers. He occasionally begins by using an existing font, sometimes referencing vintage type examples, to get the proportions correct. He also uses cut paper and stencils from time to time. Every composition is finished and coloured on the computer.

1 *A whole world under the snow*

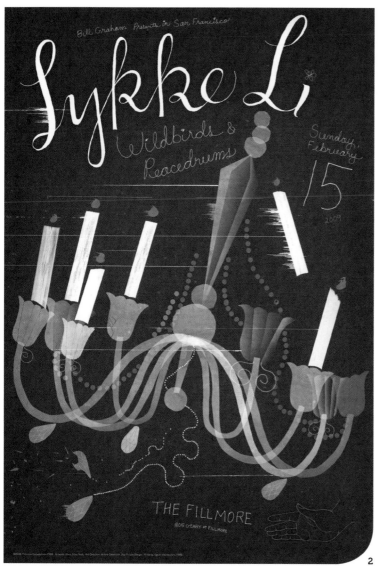

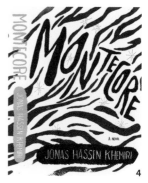

2 *Lykke Li. Wildbirds &*
Peacedrums (. . .)
3 *Pork tacos. BBQ pork*
sandwiches. Pork omelettes
4 *Montecore. Jonas*
Hassen Khemiri

JEFF CANHAM
San Francisco, California, USA

Jeff Canham is well known for his bold sign-painting and lettering work. As an apprentice at New Bohemia Signs he learnt all the traditional techniques, which he now applies to most of his art and design work. 'I use lettering quills and enamels for most of my work. My designs are often sketched out on paper, then transferred onto whatever surface I'm painting on,' Canham explains.

The two pieces shown on page 111 are from a series of pangrams (sentences containing every letter of the alphabet at least once).

The posters on page 112 were built up from painted elements that were scanned before being screenprinted. They were printed in two colours only, with overprinting used to create the additional colours.

1

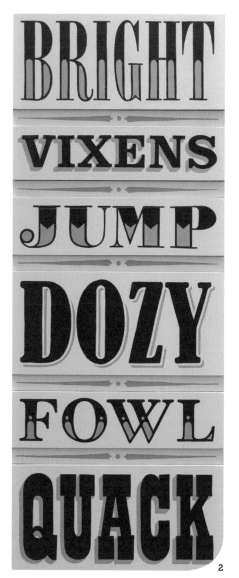

1 Alphabet

2 *Bright vixens jump dozy fowl quack*

3 *Amazingly few discotheques provide jukeboxes*

4 *The coast is clear*
5 *Save our ship!*

MIKE McQUADE
Chicago, Illinois, USA

Experimentation with materials is key to the work of Mike McQuade. In the early developmental stages of his pieces, he works in thumbnail size, which he finds easy to be creative in and which stops him from being distracted by the size of a piece.

McQuade uses a variety of materials and techniques for his work, ranging from pencil to screenprinting to other paint substrates. This particular piece was painted on tin with acrylics before being digitally retouched for print. The brief was to make certain the text was the main artwork, which offered McQuade a chance to create the kind of bold work he relishes. It was originally designed for a T-shirt, but was later made into a print.

1 *Sale. Everything is exciting! With a countdown. Only two days left!*
2 Detail

1

2

PAUL ROBSON
Newcastle upon Tyne, UK

An early love of graffiti art is what led Paul Robson (aka Muro Buro) to focus his work on lettering and type. He explains, 'Lettering to me is something that has a definite understated beauty . . . I feel I need to do my bit and help people understand that type can be beautiful.'

Robson uses Sharpie pens or finer pens to draw his letterforms and, although he does eventually photograph and digitise his work, he avoids using the computer to actually create the forms. For the smoother curves, he simply draws the letters on a large scale and, for those rougher ones, on a much smaller scale, so they have less definition when photographed.

Influenced by the work of Saul Bass, the What Can You Do series of cards on page 115 was created to promote the Northumbria University School of Design. The poster on this page was created as a self-promotional piece.

1

1 *It's complicated*
2 *Hello! Make connections.*
Make sense. Make changes
3 *Designers are going through an*
identity crisis. But what can you do?
4 Detail

GEMMA CORRELL
Norwich, Norfolk, UK

Gemma Correll describes her drawings as stream-of-consciousness doodles with the letters acting as the template for the basic outline shape. Creatures, patterns, houses and quirky landscapes are some of the elements that can be found making up the letterforms.

She says of her work, 'I think of text and image as a whole rather than as separate entities, so I enjoy hand-rendering my own lettering.'

Correll uses pen and ink straight onto paper, avoiding a multitude of pencil sketches, then uses watercolour, marker pens or digital means to add colour. All is drawn freehand, although she admits to using a ruler to keep the baseline straight.

1

2

1 *ABCDEF*
2 *It's Monday, but it's O.K!*

ALYSSA NASSNER
Forest Hill, Maryland, USA

Nassner's love of lettering is born of the freedom she finds in moving away from strict fonts and the usual conventions of typography. She explains, 'I really love the imperfections of hand lettering – there's so much more warmth and personality to hand lettering than a typeface.'

While all her work is hand-drawn initially, Nassner then uses the computer to clean up her sketches before printing them out and inking them in Micron pen. Once this stage is completed, she rescans for colouring in Photoshop. In this way, her process is very much a combination of procedures. Choose Your Own Path was finished with an old, dry brush to give textural effect.

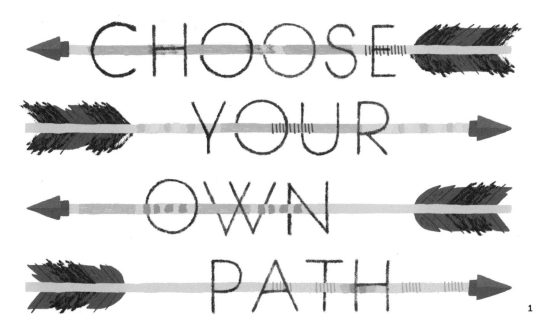

1

1 *Choose your own path*

STEVEN BURKE
Angresse, France

Steven Burke's explanation of his working process is simple. He says, 'I do a quick sketch on paper, I draw a few lines on the surface and then I paint.' He works on a broad range of surfaces, which introduces a whole new set of challenges: the smoothness of the surface or the angles of a wall, for example. At times he uses these challenges to his advantage, playing with the shapes of a wall or including wood panelling in a design.

Self-taught Burke is inspired by historical lettering. While most of the work shown here was done for personal satisfaction, it includes commissions for shops and advertising campaigns. Bicyclette For Ever is the signage of his local bike shop, while Yes Positivity Yes Yes was undertaken for Converse as part of a temporary show.

1

2

1 Yes positivity yes yes

2 Chloe's pink lemonade

3 Bicyclette for ever

4 Never ashamed

5 Always classy

JESSE HORA
Chicago, Illinois, USA

Jesse Hora is one half of MAKE.™, a Chicago-based design team specialising in art direction, print design, lettering and illustration.

The work of Hora, though hand-drawn, is incredibly detailed. He explains, 'A technique I often use when creating intricate and hand-drawn type is to lay out the lettering digitally and print out a hairline version to use as a "guide" of sorts.'

This art print was created for an exhibition. It was drawn by hand and converted into a screenprint.

1 *This is not important*

1

LETITIA BUCHAN
Melbourne, Victoria, Australia

While living and working in South Africa, Letitia Buchan was heavily influenced by the vivid colours, textures and patterns she encountered. This comes through in a positive way in all of her lettering work.

'My advice is to really explore your own styles and have fun with the process of design.' She admits, 'I don't have a certain way of creating. Often I test things out and learn what works for me through experimentation.' Unlock the Past to Enhance the Future is one of a series of self-initiated typographic prints she created to both challenge and represent herself through such experimentation.

Also shown here is one of a series of quotations surrounding themes of beauty, which was commissioned by *Peppermint* magazine. Buchan had only the spaces provided in the photographs to work with and drew inspiration from the quotes themselves to create more meaning through decoration and colour.

1

2

1 *Unlock the past to enhance the future. Celebrate life now*
2 *I know I am plus size in their terms but I am normal too (. . .)*

TEAGAN WHITE
Minneapolis, Minnesota, USA

Unlike many other practitioners, Teagan White is not drawn to lettering to further communicate a word or phrase but instead to explore the beauty and design of each individual letterform. She distorts them and combines them with imagery to create works resembling illustrations as much as letters.

She explains, 'The constraints of legibility give me a strict framework to experiment within.' Starting with loose sketches, she will then trace and add detail in small sections until the work is complete. Depending on the project, she uses a broad spectrum of materials including ink, charcoal, watercolour and pen. Braided, a work influenced by her studies of Native American typography, is painted with ink and a brush, with only the stray hairs being done with a pen.

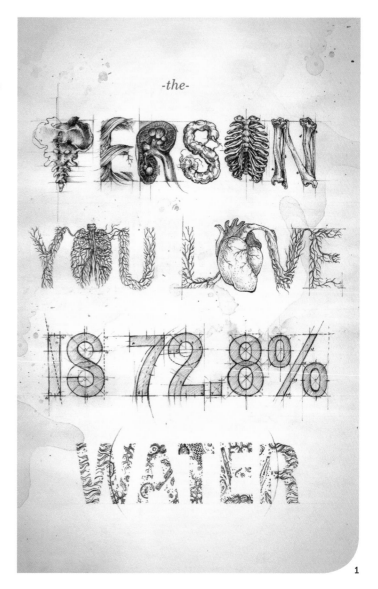

1

3

2

1 *The person you love is 72.8% water*

2 *Braided*

3 Detail

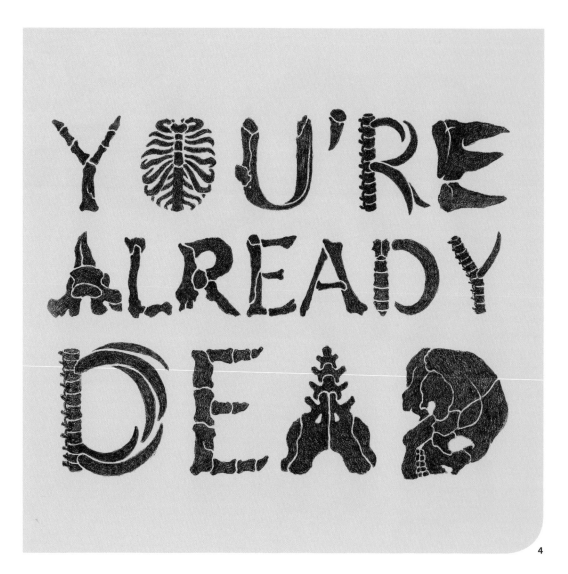

4 *You're already dead*

124 |

SLIDE SIDEWAYS
Tacoma, Washington, USA

Of primary importance to Scott and Jacqui Scoggin of Slide Sideways is maintaining an aesthetic of hand-generated work, whether tactile or in printed form. They are drawn to screenprinting for this reason as they find that transferring their hand-drawn fonts and images to a screen gives a piece of work even more of a hand-generated feel. 'A font that comes with your computer is not always the solution. Plus it's always nice to see something that's not computer-generated in an age in which technology is everywhere you look,' says Jacqui.

Heck Yes, created for the duo's online shop, began as a large-scale papercut before Slide Sideways decided to convert it to a print.

1

1 *Heck yes*

JOHN PASSAFIUME
Brooklyn, New York, USA

The Process was drafted over a three-month period as part of Passafiume's undergraduate thesis. It is the result of a hand injury, which left him temporarily unable to use the computer and having to rely on hand-generated lettering. It took over 700 hours with a Bic mechanical pencil. Process juxtaposes the qualities of hand-rendering with a digital aesthetic. In Passafiume's words, 'A needle-sharp piece of lead is essential. It is more capable and efficient than computer software, albeit difficult to master.'

Also shown here is a hand-drafted wedding announcement completed for a friend. Passafiume's digital work can be seen on page 39.

1 *Together with their families Michael Alexander Germano & Adela Laura Chipe invite your to join. Hiebfarm Shelbyville (. . .)*
2 / 3 *The Process (. . .)*

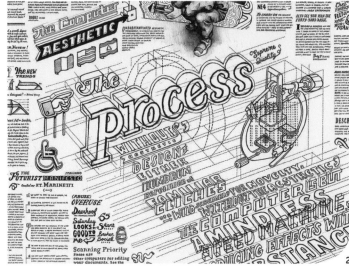

DEANNE CHEUK
New York, New York,
USA

Deanne Cheuk is both an illustrator
and an art director and says she
is drawn to lettering for both 'the
restrictions and possibilities' it brings.
Her work ranges from editorial
illustration to fine art, and her
methods of working vary greatly,
depending on the project.

Painted entirely in ink, this piece of
work uses ornate patterns and lines
to create a series of flowing and
highly illustrative letterforms. It was
completed as part of a curation
project by *Theme* magazine, for
an issue about 'Transitionists' –
designers who also work as artists.
This lettering was used throughout
the magazine for all of the headlines.

1 *Transitionists* (. . .)
2 Detail

TOM LANE
Bristol, UK

Shown here is one of 60 gorilla sculptures commissioned to celebrate Bristol Zoo's 175th birthday. Making reference to old butchers' diagrams, Tom Lane (see also page 53), in collaboration with Ged Palmer, divided the gorilla's torso up, filling the segments with facts about why gorillas are disappearing in the wild.

Lane explains, 'We created everything on the fly, without any planning or reference material. . . We were two just two guys, in a warehouse, drawing like mad from our imagination.' The entire gorilla was then sprayed with heat-sensitive black paint so the type would be gradually revealed on the surface of the gorilla throughout the day, then the surface would return to black by the cold of nightfall.

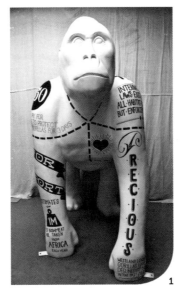

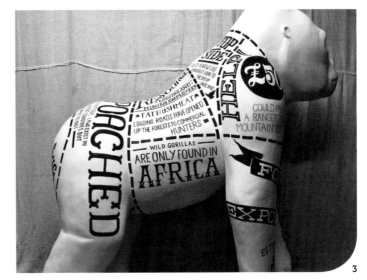

1 *Precious (. . .)*
2 *Aphrodisiac (. . .)*
3 *Wild gorillas are only found in Africa (. . .)*

CHRIS BALLASIOTES
Seattle, Washington, USA

Chris Ballasiotes became infatuated with watercolours and art while studying in Florence, Italy. He now works in a studio garage in Seattle, which gives him the space he needs to let loose on multiple projects. All the works featured here are personal projects.

Ballasiotes usually begins by brainstorming on paper with ballpoint pen or, sometimes, brush and paint. He takes inspiration from 'shapes, typography, faces, animals and anything else that might get me an idea of what I want to do'. He uses a wide variety of tools, from brushes, inks and paints to different-textured papers, tape, film cameras and printed photographs. 'I love being creative, especially with watercolours and inks. I love getting my hands dirty and mixing fun colours.'

1

2

1 *Hola, ciao, hello, bonjour, hey you (. . .)*

2 *Fortune*

3

3 *Pianos, play, pegs, open, doors, into, it,*

all, comes, together, life, relax (. . .)

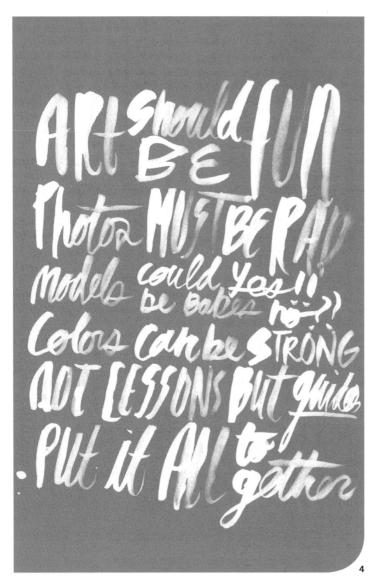

4 Art should be fun. Photos must be rad. Models could be babes. Yes!! No?? Colors can be strong. Not lessons but guides. Put it all together.

5 It's not you it's me. Lets take some time. We are better together (. . .)

6 Yes. OK. Maybe. Nope. Can I think about it. Take a rain check (. . .).

TRIBORO
Brooklyn, New York, USA

David Heasty and Stefanie Weigler of Triboro primarily work alongside clients in building their brand or identity, tackling this in many ways. They often create custom typography specifically for a project. The appeal of lettering to Triboro is that it captures both the impact and texture of an image along with a typographic message as well. Heasty believes that 'lettering is the most pure form of visual communication'.

Shown here is the CD artwork for Blonde Redhead's album *Penny Sparkle*. Although the sleeve contains no imagery, it manages to feel highly illustrative through the lettering alone. Also on this page is an invitation to a group art exhibition.

1 *Bruce Conner, George Herms, Dennis Hopper, Robert Dean Stockwell*
2 *Penny Sparkle (. . .)*

KAROLIN SCHNOOR
London, UK

Trained as an illustrator, Karolin Schnoor approaches all her lettering projects with the aim of maintaining the fluidity and freedom that her drawing also holds. She does this by writing her lettering quickly with fineliner pens to ensure the continuation of the line, then reworking over and over until it is perfect. Schnoor believes that looking at type as an illustration can be useful 'because it means you can focus on the overall balance as well as making sure it's legible'.

All the stationery examples shown here are printed using letterpress methods. The texture created by this style of printing adds to the handmade quality of the lettering.

1

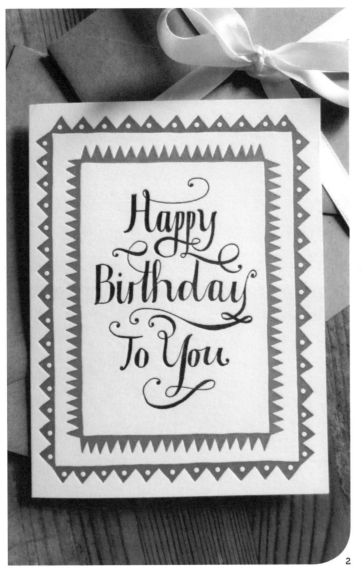

1 *Thank you so much*

2 / 3 *Happy birthday to you*

4 *Congratulations*

5 *Hugo Alexander*

LINEA CARTA
Berkeley, California, USA

Diva Pyari creates paper goods and gifts for her company, Linea Carta. Her calligraphic lettering features prominently in much of what she sells. To create her lettering, Pyari uses a dip pen with vintage nibs, such as the Nikko or the Railroad 550: nibs that are fine-tipped and firm but also quite flexible.

Pyari believes 'the real beauty of hand lettering lies in the fact that I am in each piece of it – someone else can copy the style, but there is a different nuance, a different personality, a different heart behind it'.

The tea-towel calendar shown here is redesigned on a yearly basis. It is a product that recalls the 1950s when it was very popular to collect such things. For all her work on linen, she screenprints each piece by hand.

1

2

3

4

5

6

1 *Bon appetit*

2 Linea Carta's 2011 calendar year

3 Linea Carta's 2010 calendar year

4 *Cheers*

5 *Together with their families (. . .)*

6 *Mila + Tomasso*

GEMMA O'BRIEN
Sydney, New South Wales, Australia

An eagerness to enhance communication and a passion
for drawing letterforms are the two main reasons Gemma
O'Brien works with lettering. 'I find drawing curves, looking
for relationships between particular letters and giving them
character very enjoyable,' she explains.

Once she has an idea, O'Brien begins all her works by
drawing the letters repeatedly to find relationships and
master their intricacies. From there, she develops the
textures. In some cases, she will move on to the computer.
The poster on page 139 was created for a group exhibition
and was inspired by a poem by e. e. cummings. It was
drawn small-scale, and then projected and painstakingly
redrawn large-scale, in full detail.

Script fonts are of huge inspiration to O'Brien and often
become the foundation for her type. The elegant lettering
on this birthday invitation (commissioned for former
Prime Minister of Australia Bob Hawke) uses gold foil
to add the sense of grandeur that the client required.

1 *Bob Hawke*
2 Detail
3 *Everything together carefully descending*

3

MAYBELLE IMASA-STUKULS

Oakland, California, USA

Completing a calligraphy course was the beginning of a love affair with lettering for Maybelle Imasa-Stukuls. She explains, 'I love its imperfection, that no two letters are alike. I love the human quality of it. I'm a little bit old-school in that way.' It was shortly after completing this course that her career as a calligrapher began when some of her work was featured in *Martha Stewart* magazine.

Imasa-Stukuls' love of hand lettering is so deep that she is already teaching her two-year-old twins the ways of calligraphy. The slate blackboards shown here were purchased on a trip to Paris. They are used to teach the twins their ABCs, in the hope that they, too, will appreciate the beauty and importance of hand lettering.

3

4

1 *Breakfast table civility (. . .)*

2 *L. G*

3 *Enjoy! Meet me in Paris. See you soon*

4 *Superstar. You are cute! Meet me in Paris*

JUSTIN FULLER

Boulder, Colorado, USA

As he was growing up, Justin Fuller was exposed to his father's collection of old advertising signage. He was drawn to the custom and hand-lettered typography that they displayed and remembers this experience as the first time he paid attention to anything of that kind. Those styles influence his lettering work even today.

The samples of his work shown here are for the most part commissions for music-industry clients and show references to lyrics and signage.

1

2

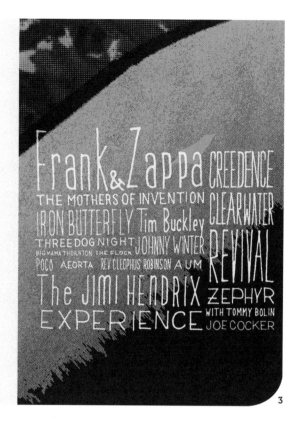

1 *Black angels*

2 *The talented Mr. Jones*

3 *Denver pop festival (. . .)*

4 *Denver music company (. . .)*

BEST DRESSED SIGNS
Boston, Massachusettes, USA

Training as an apprentice for five years with New Bohemia Signs in San Francisco, Josh Luke of Best Dressed Signs learnt all he needed to start his own sign-writing company. The process of sign writing is a complex and highly skilled one, with the application of gold leaf being especially involved. A finished sketch is translated into a paper pattern, which is then chalked onto the surface on which the sign is to be written. This chalking acts as a guide upon which to hand-render the letters with paint and brush.

'Shaping, by hand and by brush, the lines and curves of letterforms, along with creating a balance between letters, is the most challenging and rewarding part of sign painting,' says Luke.

A range of Luke's signage for tattoo parlours is showcased here, including work for some of his favourite clients (both due to their appreciation of the lettering and the tattoos they sometimes give him to pay him in kind). Circus lettering is an influence for many of these signs. Influence for Greater Boston's First and Finest is derived from Boston's paper currency and stamps of the nineteenth century. It was the first licensed tattoo parlour in Boston, and its grand and elaborate signage plays on this fact.

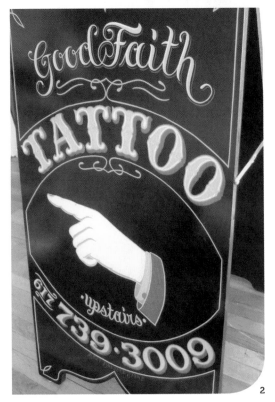

3

4

1 *Double crossed. Expert electric tattooing by Ian Oliver*

2 *Good faith tattoo upstairs (. . .)*

3 *Greater Boston's first and finest*

4 *Follow the honey*

5

6

7

5 Various letters. *Closed. 1158. Best dressed sign painters. BDS*

6 *Hand painted signs. The pre-vinylite society*

7 Detail

JAMIE LAWSON
Hamilton, Ontario, Canada

One half of creative communication duo Poly, Jamie Lawson creates both digital and hand-rendered lettering pieces. For the elaborate hand-lettering pieces shown here, his process is a fairly time-consuming one and involves using handmade stencils and layer upon layer of paint and ink. Lawson will often begin with an existing font. He explains, 'I try to combine the initial drawing with substantial, well-built typefaces that can provide a solid backbone for the stylisation I have planned.' Damn the Torpedoes is based on Futura; Cycle Tracks Will Abound in Utopia references Gotham bold.

Lawson's influences and references are far-reaching, from art movements such as Futurism and Constructivism, to various kinds of ephemera. He is drawn to lettering because of the weight words can carry and the associations and ambiguity that come with how they are presented.

Lawson's digital work can be seen on page 48.

1

2

3

4

1 *Damn the torpedoes full speed ahead*

2 Detail

3 *The fabulous night panther*

4 *Cycle tracks will abound in utopia*

Chapter 3:
Three-dimensional Lettering

Three-dimensional lettering can take many forms and use any combination of materials. The scope for experimentation far exceeds that of a paper or wall surface, but this freedom comes with its own set of challenges.

1

Some artists and designers create meticulous pieces of work using only a few materials. A sheet of paper and a scalpel, or a box of matches and some glue may be all that is needed to create something unique and extraordinary.

The unifying factor in much three-dimensional work is the extensive manual labour and time it can take to complete each piece. As with two-dimensional lettering, careful planning is vital. MaricorMaricar, for example (see pages 176–178), plot out shapes and colours on paper before beginning their final embroidery work, thus avoiding hours of unpicking mistakes. For artists using paper, however, starting from scratch is often the only option if they make a mistake or change their minds.

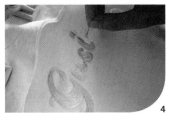

Another means of creating three-dimensional lettering is to use found objects to create letters in the environment. In these instances, photography is often the only means of documenting the final results due to their impermanence. By using objects familiar to everyone, but recontextualising them, a new level of interest and communication is acheived. By using flaming firelighters as a material for one of his pieces, Dominic Le-Hair (see pages 170–171) not only creates an engaging piece of work but also adds to the meaning of the message.

A common problem for practitioners creating three-dimensional type is resolving legibility issues while still pushing form. We are all taught the shape of letters on a flat surface, but the distortion of these letters into a physical three-dimensional plane can sometimes cause problems. Trial and error is really the only way to get around this, and many of the practitioners featured on the following pages have become experts in their particular material of choice as a direct result of this.

1 Bianca Chang layers hand-cut sheets to construct her letterforms
2 Shown here is a selection of the tools Bianca Chang uses to create her carved paper letters (see pages 156–157)
3 / 4 MaricorMaricar (see pages 176–178) begin with sketches before moving on to embroider their lettering

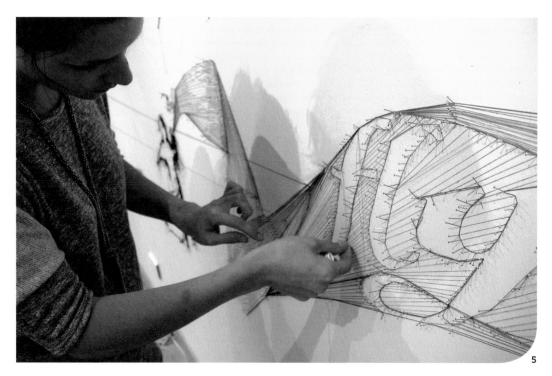

5

6

Photographing three-dimensional work is something that often requires consideration, as many commissioned lettering projects are destined to be featured in either print publications or other such two-dimensional planes. It is vital that the photography captures the texture and uniqueness of the three-dimensional material, yet that it is still legible and able to translate well enough to stand up against any digitally produced equivalents. Intricate camera set-ups are required for this in many cases as, without attention to this detail, the impact of a whole project could be ruined. However, when done well, the photographs will bring out the distinct textural beauty of a piece of work, and the materials used will be on full show.

TOOLS

Due to the experimental nature of three-dimensional lettering, the tools used vary greatly from practitioner to practitioner and are too numerous to describe in full here. However, three vital pieces of equipment, across the board, are the following:

Camera

A DSLR camera provides the greatest flexibility and control when photographing work. Being able to control the shutter speed and aperture, especially when the lighting is good, gives you a better chance of capturing a perfect representation.

Tripod

For capturing work more precisely and ensuring a blur-free image, a tripod can be a very useful tool.

Adobe Photoshop (or equivalent)

Photo-editing software is essential for touching up photographs or cropping into individual letterforms.

7

5 Debbie Smyth (see pages 158–159) uses pins and string to construct her lettering works. Many of her projects are temporary installation works and require photographic documentation

6 Vladimir Končar photographs each carefully constructed letter individually, creating words in Photoshop afterwards (see page 184)

7 For many of Owen Gildersleeve's lettering projects, the photography of the final three-dimensional model is as important as the work itself (see pages 164–165)

YULIA BRODSKAYA
London, UK

Yulia Brodskaya is well known for her signature style of intricate and colourful three-dimensional lettering. She explains her love of the 'endless field for creativity' that comes from illustrating letters, rather than using a typeface. She feels that, with the addition of pictorial elements and the use of different materials, lettering becomes more than just a word.

The technique Brodskaya uses is quilling, which involves rolling strips of coloured paper and gluing them onto a paper or card background. Shown here is a range of projects, commissioned by various international clients, that Brodskaya created using this technique. While all her projects begin with very precise planning sketches, there is often room for some experimentation when the actual paperwork begins, so new ideas can come to life.

(PENGUIN CLASSICS)RED

WILLIAM THACKERAY
Vanity Fair

1

2

3

1 *I'm no angel.*
William Thackeray. Vanity Fair
2 *Flourish*
3 *100 dollars*
4 4 *The gift shop*

BIANCA CHANG
Sydney, New South Wales, Australia

Bianca Chang's works are the product of precision, patience and a degree of mathematical problem solving. She explains, 'Being able to measure and plot effectively is especially helpful. To me, this is 70 per cent of the job – cutting skills are secondary.' Once sketched and plotted, Chang cuts sheets of paper by hand, in angled increments. Placing these sheets in a stack creates a hollowed-out letterform. Some pieces comprise over 200 cut sheets of paper.

Both of the pieces presented here were created as part of a paper exhibition held in Sydney, the brief for which was simply, 'create with paper'.

Chang explains the thinking behind Twin. 'I was inspired by the lettering used in the scoreboards of old video games – no curves, only pixels. The letters are strikingly minimal.' PS was inspired by retro geometric letterpress forms. It is based on an alphabet constructed only with rectangles, triangles and circles.

1

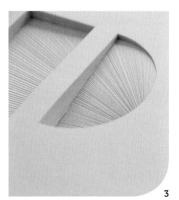

3

4

2

1 *Twin*
2 *PS*
3 / 4 Detail

DEBBIE SMYTH
Stroud, UK

With a background in contemporary textiles, Debbie Smyth works only with dressmaking pins, a hammer and a multitude of coloured threads to make ornate and textured lettering works. From a distance, they may sometimes look like a mass of knots but, on closer inspection, the sharp edges of the letterforms are revealed.

She plans each composition on the computer, then transfers it to a wall or board before pinning, then wrapping the thread around the pins. Smyth explains, 'The drawing often changes quite a lot at this point, as it is more material-led.'

Fly Away Home, commissioned for a textile festival, was installed on-site. Smyth used the large wall space of the museum to construct a fluid piece, choosing flowing script and calligraphic fonts. She included hand-cut lettering to add contrast to the textile elements.

1

2

1 *h. e. V. O. x. D. j. L*
2 *Fly away home*
spread your wings and fly,
Take the beauty of your soul
and share it with the sky
3 Detail

3

PEI-SAN NG
Chicago, Illinois, USA

An architect by trade, Pei-San Ng began making artworks a few years ago upon moving to Chicago. The three-dimensional match piece shown here is based around ideas of combustibility, destruction and burning, with the full series of work including lettering pieces as well as other icons and images.

The lettering for all of Ng's work is based on her own strictly structured three-line cursive handwriting. She explains, 'I believe in the beauty of everyone's unique handwriting. Even if it looks like a chicken scratch, it's beautiful because it's an extension of a person's thought/being. I want this message to come from me.'

Once the letters are sketched, they will then be transferred onto wood using carbon paper. She overlays a grid guide and begins gluing matches until all spaces are filled and the solid three-dimensional structure is complete.

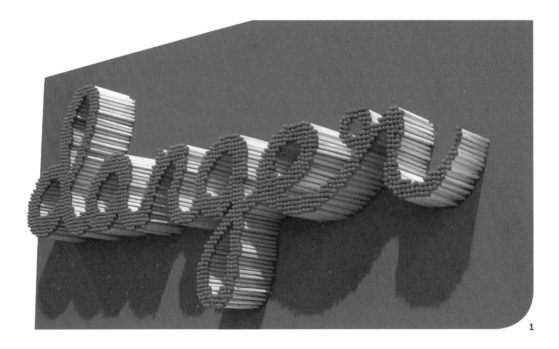

1

1 *Danger*

JAMES T EDMONDSON
San Francisco, California, USA

James T Edmondson views himself as a graphic designer who often uses lettering. He takes pleasure in creating inventive three-dimensional projects that only come together in the final stages.

Aged Beef was created for the party of a friend of his whose nickname is Beef Nugget, hence the title. The letterforms were created from red cups, as they are an integral part of any college party. Each cup had to be partially filled with water in order to prevent it from blowing away. After the piece was captured on film, the cups were washed and used for the party.

1

1 *127 Albion presents aged beef*

ERIK MARINOVICH

Brooklyn, New York, USA

The lettering on this page is the result of Erik Marinovich's discovery, during a spring clean, of a mound of shredded paper that had been steadily growing for some time. He explains, 'I figured it could potentially be used to make lettering. I quickly converted my kitchen into a photo studio and began to sculpt letters from the paper and document it.' Due to space constraints, photographs were taken a letter or two at a time before the phrase was finally composited in Photoshop.

Marinovich constantly experiments with both materials and the crafting of letterforms to make dynamic and original lettering examples. Such experimentation is also shown in his hand-generated work (see page 85).

1 *Ready, set, make!*

1

BENJA HARNEY
Sydney, New South Wales, Australia

Working exclusively with paper, Benja Harney creates all manner of sculptures, pop-up books and constructions. A self-taught paper engineer, he describes the lure of paper as being in the contradictions it presents – it is both strong and delicate, complex and simple.

Harney explains, 'When working with paper, one has to make and remake something many times, overcoming design challenges along the way until perfection is reached.'

A4, shown here, was completed by Harney as part of an alphabet-specific exhibition and pop-up shop in Sydney. Made using only mounted red card, the work is composed of four extruded A letterforms.

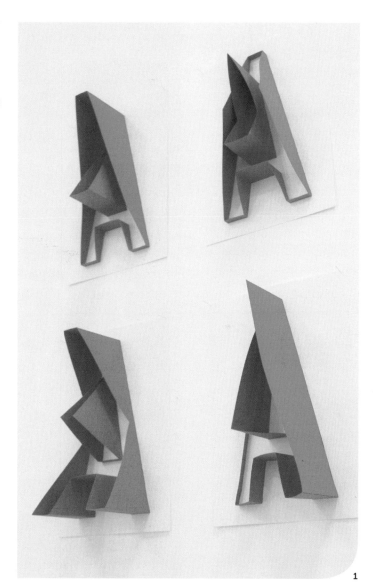

1 *A*

1

OWEN GILDERSLEEVE
London, UK

'I really enjoy being given a piece of copy and then trying to find an interesting way of creating an illustration that both complements the text and brings it to life.'

Owen Gildersleeve is well known for his paper-cut pieces, for which he uses a scalpel to cut into layers of coloured paper and card. He reveals, 'I generally draw out my lettering backwards onto the reverse of the paper so that, when they're cut out, there are no marks visible.'

A challenging and time-consuming aspect of his process is photographing the end product, which he often does himself, retouching and editing the image to ensure that all colours and textures are accurate. All of the pieces shown here were created first as three-dimensional hand-crafted pieces and then photographed to be used for print.

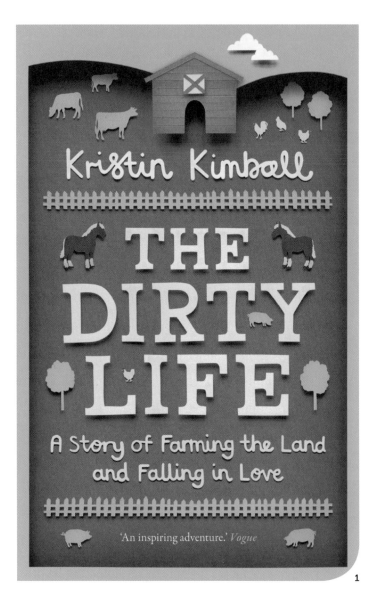

1

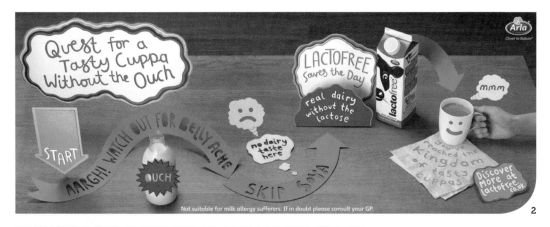

2

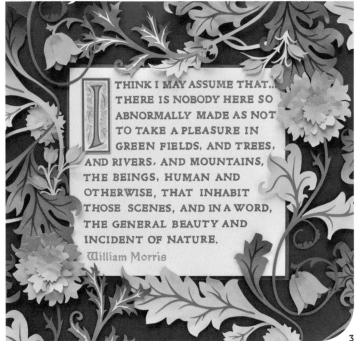

3

1 *Kristin Kimball. The dirty life. A story of farming the land and falling in love (. . .)*

2 *Quest for a tasty cuppa without the ouch. Lactofree saves the day. You've reached the kingdom of tasty cuppas (. . .)*

3 *I think I may assume that . . . there is nobody here so abnormally made as not to take a pleasure in green fields, (. . .) William Morris*

TRIBORO
Brooklyn, New York, USA

The team at Triboro try to disguise the materials and processes they use as much as possible, enjoying the result when these are not identifiable. 'No materials or techniques are off-limits. Often we tinker and experiment with whatever is lying around,' says David Heasty.

Heasty explains, 'Usually, as we are experimenting with whatever process we are using, we'll make a mistake or an observation that will take us in a direction we would never have anticipated. The unpredictability inherent in the process is what is so entertaining for us.'

1 *Ten cents on the dollar*

2 *Otherwise amazing*

3 *Tilt*

1

2

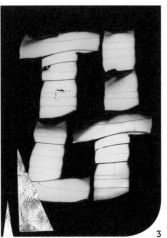

3

NINA GREGIER
Krakow, Poland

Using brightly coloured cotton thread, Nina Gregier embroiders bold geometric letterforms onto black card. First plotting the letters on graph paper or drawing them out in Illustrator, she will then make small holes in the card to accommodate the thread. The embroidery itself is a time-consuming task, but one that she finds relaxing.

The letterforms themselves are kept as simple as possible, using only a few shapes to give the outline. Two lengths of line and one angle, for example, is all that may be required. This minimalist rigour presents challenges in legibility for Gregier, but it is a challenge she more often than not overcomes in the end.

1

3

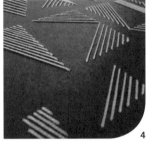

4

2

1 *Some*

2 Alphabet

3 / 4 Details

DOMINIC LE-HAIR
Peterborough, UK

The use of materials not normally associated with type and lettering is a trademark of Dominic Le-Hair's lettering work. Firelighters and iron filings, as shown here, are some examples of this. Le-Hair enjoys looking at objects and questioning if and how they could be used to create something typographic.

Firelighter Type (right) was a personal project inspired by waiting for a barbecue to heat up. Picking up a firelighter block, Le-Hair noticed how easily it crumbled and wondered if it would carve well. He created the letters and superglued them onto a piece of scrap wood that was painted black. In the dark, he put a match to it, and the flames shot up. He took as many photographs, from as many different angles, as possible.

Magnetic Type (far right), another personal project, was created using magnets and iron filings.

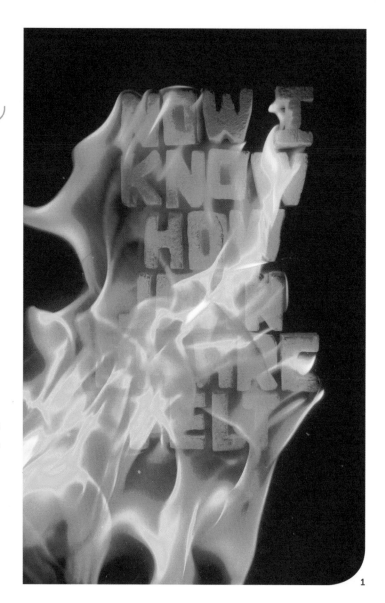

1

2

3

4

1 *Now I know how Joan of Arc felt*
2 *Even if love were not what
I wanted . . . love would make love
the thing most desired*
3 / 4 Details

CHARLES WILLIAMS
London, UK

Charles Williams identifies the two most important tools of his trade as an obsessive enjoyment in creating things by hand and lots of patience.

Using pencils, drawing pens and paper to sketch out a concept, he then moves on to Illustrator to finalise the idea. For the works shown here, foam board, pins, glue and paint were used to create a structure based on the digital work. Finally, Williams photographed the pieces and then treated the image in Photoshop, adding colour and removing any unwanted elements.

In the piece Go Play, the design and colours hint at American sports, outdoors, fields and landscapes. Williams designed the font using the organic and geometric shapes around it as a guide. Gloss acrylic was used to give the whole piece a varnished feel.

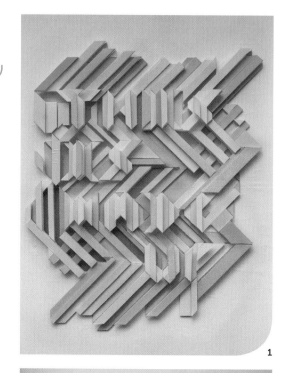

1

2

1 *This is made up*
2 *Go play*

SCISSORS
Sydney, New South Wales, Australia / London, UK

A design and art collective that tries to avoid the computer as much as possible, Scissors aims to work with tangible materials, using techniques such as origami, as shown in this work. The brief for this identity for an animation festival was to create something very colourful and memorable based on a strong concept associated with theoretical aspects of animation. Scissors took inspiration from the Muybridge Horse in Motion, one of the first examples of breaking down something sequentially and looking closely at each frame, but made it more vibrant to reflect the playful nature of the animation festival. Everything for this animated piece was done completely in-camera.

1 *UTS: Sydney International Animation Festival 10. 24–26 Sept*

1

AMANDINE ALESSANDRA
London, UK

Whereas many practitioners aim to enhance the meaning of the text through their lettering, Amandine Alessandra prefers to interfere with it. 'Using images or objects to build up words can enhance or corrupt their interpretation and say a lot more than what is written,' she explains. Her passion lies in finding alternatives to print and digital communication, resulting in her three-dimensional typographic installations. Her letters play and interact with the scene in which they are set, providing an element of suprise and, she hopes, eliciting a smile.

This piece, which plays on a quote from Lewis Carroll, uses the grid of the fence to weave the letters in fluorescent pink wool.

1 *I have proved by actual trial that a letter that takes an hour to write takes only three minutes to read!*

1

ANDREW
BYROM
Long Beach, California, USA

'The move to a three-dimensional approach was born from a desire to move out of my comfort zone and force myself to create or build letters from a new standpoint.'

The work of Andrew Byrom is a reaction to the processes and materials that often force the outcome of a design. His use of three-dimensional materials, while adhering to typographic principles (such as x-height, structure, etc) is made more challenging by the need to address architectural aspects. For example, the table and stools shown here, spelling out UCLA, must be legible as text while still having the physical strength to hold those who sit at them.

In most cases, the idea comes first for Byrom, with choice of materials following. Often his experiments find their way back to more traditional two-dimensional type designs.

EXTENSION

WINTER QUARTER 2012 January 9th – April 1st

1

2

1 *UCLA (. . .)*
2 Detail

MARICORMARICAR
London, UK

A focus on hand-crafted design is what twin sisters Maricor and Maricar set out to achieve when in 2010 they decided to work together. They create works that are playful, both in material and through the words they choose.

To create their embroidered lettering, as shown here, they use plain-weave fabric and cotton embroidery thread, as well as a selection of hoops and frames.

Planning is an essential stage of their process, and they begin with sketches before choosing colours. They explain, 'We use watercolours very loosely when we work up sketches for our embroidery and find that we come across interesting colour combinations that way, almost by accident.'

Apart from Go Play, which was commissioned by *ESPN The Magazine*, all the work shown here was self-initiated, for exhibiting. Go Play was inspired by the patterns and textures of the cosy knitted sweaters of Norway and coloured accordingly using Illustrator.

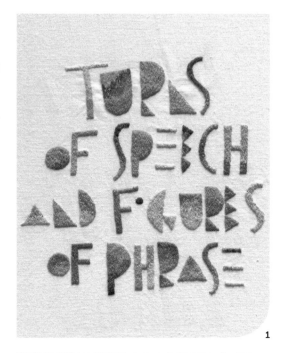

1

2

1 *Turns of speech and figures of phrase*
2 *Tongue-tied & hopeless*
3 *Muscle on*
4 *Go play*

5 *Macho distrust*

6 / 7 Details

JULENE HARRISON
Worthing, UK

Paper cutting is an age-old art form first developed in China soon after the invention of paper, and later spreading to the rest of the world.

Although Julene Harrison bases her paper-cut lettering on previously existing fonts, she manipulates and cuts into the letters to give them character and to intertwine them into her decorative illustrations. First developing her compositions in Photoshop, she next prints out the design in reverse onto an oversized sheet of paper. She painstakingly cuts out each detail and ensures that every part is attached to another, resulting in one complete but very delicate piece of work.

1

1 *Tea glorious tea!*

KATE FORRESTER
Brighton, UK

Redrawing her letters many times, first by hand and then on the computer, Kate Forrester goes back and forth between the two methods until the letters are perfectly refined. For her paper cuts, she then uses a laser-cutting machine, preferring the smooth curves to those of a scalpel.

She especially enjoys a brief that specifies the mood the letters should convey. 'I enjoy making words appear "decadent" or "Baroque" or "joyful" or "creepy",' she explains. The lettering for the Moonstruck chocolate project shown here was to look organic and delicious. In designing for the actual chocolate mould, Forrester needed to also consider how the chocolate would break.

The alphabet series shown here weaves imagery together to make up the body of the letters while not allowing the swirls and illustrations to distract from the letterforms. They were created as pieces for sale in her online shop.

1

2

1 *Share if you dare*

2 *Moonstruck. Venezuela /*
Dominican Republic (. . .)

3 *S / It's all in her mind*

4 / 5 *Various letters*

ARIANE SPANIER
Berlin, Germany

'Letters are what we can "own" as designers aside from whatever content there might be in a book, on a poster, etc. Lettering also provides a way of illustrating without actually using an image other than the letters.'

Ariane Spanier is a designer who creates lettering using traditional materials such as paper, pens and computer software, but also employing more unorthodox materials such as hair, string, rice and, recently, clay.

For Body Wash, the type was created from soap as an illustration for the *New York Times Magazine*. The article was about how the word 'soap' has, over time, been replaced by the phrase 'body wash'.

The So Wird's Gemacht poster was created for a seminar with the artist Karin Sander and her students. In this piece, the letterforms are constructed by the negative space created by an arrangement of different tools and art materials.

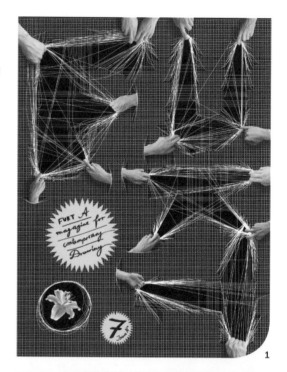

1

1 *Fukt. A magazine for contemporary drawing*
2 Detail

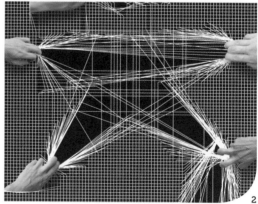

2

3

4

5

3 *Body wash*
4 *Fukt magazine: magazine for drawing*
5 *How it's done (. . .)*

VLADIMIR KONČAR

Zagreb, Croatia

'As children we were taught how to read and write and, as we grew older, we stopped noticing the differences in form and concentrated on the messages letters carry. When I started going into the details of certain fonts, I started enjoying those details and letter shapes.'

The pieces shown here are from Vladimir Končar's Diary Type project, a self-initiated series using a wide variety of materials. This emerged from daily ideas that he noted down. He then worked on ways to visualise them to create symbolic links between font and thought.

Using a small table as the working surface, Končar laid out each letter before photographing the piece, editing in Photoshop.

1 *Little things amaze me*

2 *Z*

1

2

JEROME HALDEMANN
Leysin, Switzerland

This alphabet was created by Jerome Haldemann as part of a university assignment. The brief was to create a font inspired by a specific animal, and the inspirational animal here was the hedgehog. Based on the existing typeface Bodoni, it is made up of toothpicks pushed into foam board at varying angles. No glue or bonding agents were used.

One of the most challenging aspects of this project was the photography. The letters needed to be shot individually, but from the same angle, to ensure legibility and consistency in the shadows.

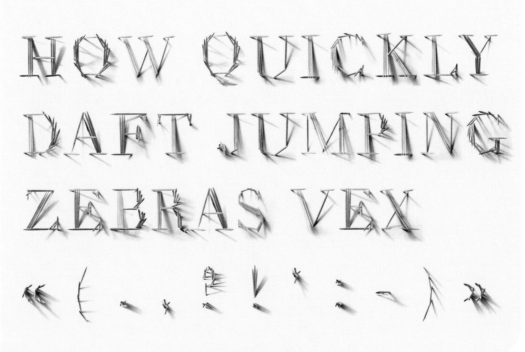

1

1 *How quickly daft jumping zebras vex.* (Punctuation marks)

CONTRIBUTORS

Esther Aarts
http://www.estheraarts.nl

Simon Ålander
http://www.coffeemademedoit.com

Amandine Alessandra
http://www.amandinealessandra.com

Chris Ballasiotes
http://www.siotes.com

Marian Bantjes
http://www.bantjes.com

André Beato
http://www.andrebeato.com

Best Dressed Signs
http://bestdressedsigns.com

Steven Bonner
http://www.stevenbonner.com

Yulia Brodskaya
http://www.artyulia.com

Letitia Buchan
http://www.letitiabuchan.com

Steven Burke
http://www.stevenburke.org

Andrew Byrom
http://andrewbyrom.com

Joey Camacho
http://www.joeycamacho.com

Jeff Canham
http://www.jeffcanham.com

Aaron Carámbula
http://www.friendsoftype.com

Dan Cassaro
http://youngjerks.com

Bianca Chang
http://biancachang.com

Deanne Cheuk
http://www.deannecheuk.com

Jon Contino
http://joncontino.com

Gemma Correll
http://www.gemmacorrell.com

Craig&Karl
http://craigandkarl.com

Jim Datz
http://www.neitherfishnorfowl.com

Danielle Davis
http://www.danielleishere.com

Keetra Dean Dixon
http://www.fromkeetra.com

James T Edmondson
http://jamestedmondson@gmail.com

Carson Ellis
http://www.carsonellis.com

Alonzo Felix
http://cargocollective.com/alonzofelix

Kate Forrester
http://www.kateforrester.co.uk

Sean Freeman
http://www.thereis.co.uk

Justin Fuller
http://www.pencilpluspaper.com
http://www.goodappl.es

Owen Gildersleeve
http://www.owengildersleeve.com

Nina Gregier
http://www.ninagregier.com

Jerome Haldemann
http://be.net/jerome_haldemann

Benja Harney
http://paperform.wordpress.com

Julene Harrison
http://madebyjulene.com

Adam Hill
http://www.velcrosuit.com

Jessica Hische
http://www.jessicahische.is

Geoffrey Holstad
http://sosweaty.tumblr.com

Jesse Hora
http://www.readysetmake.com

Linzie Hunter
http://www.linziehunter.co.uk

ilovedust
http://www.ilovedust.com

Maybelle Imasa-Stukuls
http://www.may-belle.com

Andrew Joyce
http://www.doodlesandstuff.com

Sarah King
http://www.sarahaking.com

Vladimir Končar
http://www.koncar.info

Tom Lane
http://www.gingermonkeydesign.com

Jamie Lawson
http://polystudio.ca
http://jamielawsonart.com

Dominic Le-Hair
http://www.behance.net/

Seb Lester
http://www.seblester.co.uk

Linea Carta
http://www.linea-carta.com

Luke Lucas
http://www.lukelucas.com

Josh Luke
http://bestdressedsigns.com

Matt Lyon
http://www.c8six.com

MaricorMaricar
http://www.maricormaricar.com

Erik Marinovich
http://www.friendsoftype.com

Mary Kate McDevitt
http://www.marykatemcdevitt.com

McFadden & Thorpe
http://www.macfaddenandthorpe.com

Grady McFerrin
http://www.gmillustration.com

Mike McQuade
http://mikemcquade.com

Drew Melton
http://www.yourjustlucky.com
http://phrasologyproject.com

Ed Nacional
http://www.ednacional.com

Alyssa Nassner
http://alyssanassner.com

Christopher Silas Neal
http://redsilas.com

Pei-San Ng
http://peisanng.com

Gemma O'Brien
http://www.fortheloveoftype.com.au

Mats Ottdal
http://www.jeksel.com

John Passafiume
http://johnpassafiume.com

Dennis Payongayong
http://www.friendsoftype.com

People Collective
http://www.peoplecollective.com.au

Richard Perez
http://skinnyships.com

Sasha Prood
http://www.sashaprood.com

Dado Queiroz
http://dadoqueiroz.com

Paul Robson
http://www.muro-buro.com

Jeff Rogers
http://www.frogers.net

Karolin Schnoor
http://www.karolinschnoor.co.uk

Scissors
http://www.scissors.cc

Skyrill
http://www.skyrill.com

Slide Sideways
http://www.slide-sideways.com

Andy Smith
http://www.asmithillustration.com

Timba Smits
http://www.timbasmits.com

Debbie Smyth
http://www.debbie-smyth.com
http://www.debbiesmyth.blogspot.com

Ariane Spanier
http://www. arianespanier.com

Liam Stevens
http://www.liamstevens.com

Michal Sycz
http://www.noeeko.com

Dana Tanamachi
http://www.danatanamachi.com

Kelly Thorn
http://www.coroflot.com/
    kellymelissathorn

Jim Tierney
jimtierneyart.com

Toby & Pete
www.tobyandpete.com

Triboro
www.triborodesign.com

Jaime Van Wart
ketchup-mustard.com

Teagan White
www.teaganwhite.com

Charles Williams
www.madeup.org

Nate Williams
www.n8w.com

Jason Wong
www.friendsoftype.com
enormouschampion.com

INDEX

ACKNOWLEDGEMENTS

Thank you to all the artists and designers who have so
generously contributed their lettering work to this book.
It has been such a treat to discover so many talented people
and even more fantastic to receive such a great response
from everyone.

I also want to thank the most excellent team at RotoVision
for this great opportunity; Isheeta and Lindy for their
support and guidance, Emily and Rebecca for designing
the book so beautifully.

Last but not least, thank you to my amazing husband, Jon,
for his expert eyes, attentive ears and general patience with
my completing of this book.

This book is for our new little creation, Leo.